Neve
CAMPBELL

AN UNAUTHORIZED BIOGRAPHY

Neve
CAMPBELL

AN UNAUTHORIZED BIOGRAPHY

ELINA FURMAN

RENAISSANCE BOOKS

Los Angeles

Library of Congress Catalog Card Number: 99-067636
ISBN: 1-58063-126-6

10 9 8 7 6 5 4 3 2 1

Design by Tanya Maiboroda

Published by Renaissance Books
Distributed by St. Martin's Press
Manufactured in the United States of America

First Edition

For Mom

Acknowledgments

I'd like to thank everyone who helped me put this book together, including my editor, Jim Parish, for all his effort and dedication, Peter Rubie for thinking of me for the project, and Giles Anderson. As always, my mother, Mira, was a constant source of ideas and moral support. And none of this could have been possible without my sister Leah. She was a tremendous help in bringing this project to completion. Finally, I would like to thank John Nikkah and Brenda Scott Royce for providing invaluable research assistance.

Contents

YOUNG PIONEER

rains, beauty, talent. These words have been used to describe Neve Campbell on countless occasions. But three words alone could never define the discreet charm that has propelled this Canadian import into the hearts of millions. For her work in the thriller *Scream 2* (1997), Neve won the Blockbuster and MTV Movie Awards for best actress (upsetting *Titanic*'s Kate Winslet, among other favorites). At the 1998 Academy Awards ceremony in Los Angeles, Neve sparkled alongside such other glamorous presenters as Cameron Diaz and Ashley Judd. It seems as though every other month finds her on the cover of some national magazine. And, judging by the amount of coverage she receives on TV's *Entertainment Tonight* and *Access Hollywood*, people are just as enamored with Neve as ever. The public has good reason to be so smitten, after all, a multidimensional, often paradoxical personality such as Neve Campbell's deserves to be celebrated.

But what can you say about a girl who was branded a "loser" in high school and went on to win over a nation? What can you say about a self-professed teenage ugly duckling who now graces the covers of fashion magazines? What can you say about a daughter who struggled with her parents' divorce only to become a veritable child bride by marrying her high school sweetheart? What can you say about a ballerina who abandoned the world of dance, referring to its climate as "backstabbing," only to enter the highly competitive realm of acting?

To dismiss these paradoxes would mean to never really know Neve Campbell, whose personal and professional struggles have shaped her into one of the most fascinating personalities in show business today. Inconsistencies have a way of creeping into every person's life. Yet few people can parlay the underpinnings of their human complexity into viable commodities as effortlessly as Neve. Almost unconsciously, the striking young actress has drawn upon her difficult past to create a public persona rife with nuances, subtleties, and riddles.

Some would say she is a crafty business woman; others would say she is one of the new breed of young stars (a group that includes such actresses as Katie Holmes, Sarah Michelle Gellar, and Jennifer Love Hewitt) riding Hollywood's teensploitation wave. At the heart of Neve Campbell the celebrity lies a series of contradictions that has catapulted her from tormented schoolgirl to television icon and, finally, to much-beloved and respected film star.

"Ms. Campbell, is there any truth to the rumor that your marriage broke up because of your husband's professional jealousy?"

"How does it feel to be called the next Jamie Lee Curtis?"

"Are you tired of playing good-girl roles like Julia Salinger?"

Whenever Neve Campbell ventures out of her Hollywood Hills home these days, bedecked in regalia worthy of an Oscar night, such questions are bound to erupt from the overeager throng of entertainment gossip mongers. All such queries are just as sure to elicit a pat "no comment" from the guarded young actress.

"Excuse me, but who are you?" is one question Neve rarely hears, whether she's at the Oscars, the Emmys, the Golden Globes, or the MTV Movie Awards. The winsome ingenue, who is currently helping to set international box-office records, is instantly recognizable when making the public scene. It's only when she steps out of her starlet role that Neve can pass virtually unnoticed through the crowded Los Angeles streets. Underneath the professional hair and makeup lies an ordinary girl next-door. No matter what look Neve may be sporting in the movie-of-the-moment or event-du-jour, her baggy-old-sweater-loving personality shines through.

Neve Campbell looks tired. As one of Hollywood's hottest and most in-demand actresses, she hardly has time in her hectic daily schedule to shower, much less make time for a press junket. Yet that's exactly what she winds up doing, as entertainment journalists from all over the country have been flown in especially for this occasion. With hordes waiting their turn to interview the reigning princess of all things teen about her latest film outing, Neve can sense that this is going to be a long day. Even with a scant ten minutes allocated for each of the scoop hounds, she's still not going to make it home by sundown.

As her publicist hovers in the background, Neve discusses the usual media subjects with practiced ease. Yes, it's true, she was the object of much ridicule in grammar school. And yes, she did aspire to be a dancer—still does as a matter of fact. No, she won't be leaving *Party of Five* any time soon. Inquiring minds want to know all about her, and Neve is not shy about giving out the details—when they don't reveal too much about her highly classified private life.

Shyness is something Neve—now in her mid-twenties—has long since outgrown. After all, as opposed to that of most of her onscreen personae, Campbell's adolescence is a thing of the distant past. Neve is an international star and a huge box-office draw. The show that made her famous won a Golden Globe for best television drama in January 1996. She's been a presenter at the Oscars and recipient at the MTV Movie Awards, where she is a perennial favorite. No wonder Hollywood studio executives told *Premiere* magazine, "She's on the top of our casting lists."

Enjoying the sweet smell of success, the actress looks poised and ready to tackle any challenge, even obtrusive reporters. Meanwhile, her crack team of press agents stands at the ready, only too willing to cut any and all interviews short should they stray from business topics and into Neve's personal matters. Considering that just a few years ago Neve couldn't even get a job on TV's *Baywatch*, it's amazing how far she's come.

Since Neve's 1994 Hollywood landing, she has staked a claim as the forerunner of the teen-power movement that is still sweeping the entertainment industry. Had it not been for her painfully honest portrayal of brainy and beautiful Julia Salinger on the hit Fox series *Party of Five* (1994–present), television and film very well may have remained in the dark ages where teenagers are concerned. Contemporary television, save for ABC's critically acclaimed dramatic series *My So-Called Life* (1994–96), had precious little to offer young adults before *Party of Five* came along. Neve Campbell's hyper-authentic personification of the teen struggle has made her the voice of the new generation. And in an age dominated by the youth culture, that's quite a coup.

Party of Five was one of the first teen-centered TV melodramas to take itself seriously. Neve's gripping portrayal of problem-plagued Julia Salinger validated the angst with which all adolescents grapple. No longer did junior audiences feel the need to make fun of their nighttime TV entertainment. While such Fox television shows as *Beverly Hills, 90210* (1990–present) and *Melrose Place* (1992–99) gained a following on the basis of their high "tune in and tune out" factor, few members of the target audience could admit to watching without suffering twinges of guilt and embarrassment. Today smart, youth-oriented prime-time fare, such as *Dawson's Creek* (1998–present), *Buffy the Vampire Slayer* (1997–present), and *Felicity* (1998–present), is becoming more prevalent with each successive season.

While Neve may not have been solely responsible for introducing the 1990s to the intelligent and introspective teen, she has given this concept a realistic archetype in Julia Salinger, as well as her various big-screen characterizations.

Prior to 1996's *Scream*, teen horror flicks were hardly the vehicles of choice for rising movie stars. The early 1980s had seen a proliferation of low-budget, low-grossing gore fests such as *Halloween* (1978), *Prom Night* (1980), *Friday the 13th* (1980), and *Nightmare on Elm Street* (1984). However, when Neve played the tough and quick-witted Sidney Prescott in *Scream*, her character's blatant girl-power struck a strong chord with impressionable young audiences.

In choosing to pursue creator Kevin Williamson's razor-sharp *Scream*, Neve had made the smartest decision of her acting career to date. Yet, by making the project, Neve was putting her reputation as a serious actress on the line. Many people—including some of Neve's most trusted colleagues—questioned her judgment. "I wouldn't have suggested that career move," said Amy Lippman, executive producer of *Party of Five*.

But as Neve read the page-turner of a script, she realized that *Scream* was no ordinary thriller. The fine dialogue and character development suggested that this was a drastic departure from the stereotypes and gratuitous violence of the much-maligned slasher genre. "For me, it's always dependent on the character and the script," said the shrewd young actress. "I look beyond what's on the page."

With such remarkable foresight in picking great roles, Neve may very well have been looking into a crystal ball. *Scream* went on to strike box-office gold with $103 million in gross ticket sales, becoming the highest-grossing horror entry ever made. The blockbuster movie made Neve a household name. More importantly, it persuaded Hollywood that intelligent youth is not a myth perpetrated by unemployed screenwriters, but is in fact an ever-present reality.

A new, more youth-friendly era has dawned upon the media, and Neve Campbell is to be congratulated for helping to bring it about. This unlikely pioneer is actually a brown-haired, brown-eyed everygirl. At five-foot-five and one-half inches, and approximately 115 pounds, Neve hardly cuts an imposing figure. Sweetness and hospitality are her trademark traits. A far cry from a tortured artist, Neve is as mild-mannered and even-tempered as divas come.

The child of a broken family, this Canadian export endured her own personal hell while still a schoolgirl. Mocked and tormented throughout her school years, she grew accustomed to the role of outsider. To this day, she does not expect either audiences or her peers to welcome her with open arms. Since she still is amazed by the robust proportions of her fan mail bags, Neve stands in no danger of becoming complacent.

Neve's broad appeal comes as no surprise to her mother, who is the president of her daughter's ever-growing fan club. With the unflagging support of her family, Neve has wound up a winner in the cutthroat showbiz game. To prevail, she's had to endure work weeks that would make Wall Street stockbrokers beg for mercy. As a result, she has had to all but forfeit any hope of a personal life in the imminent future. Through it all she's managed to don a courageous facade for her public. Unlike many spoiled and self-absorbed actors of today's generation, Neve has made a career out of taking risks, challenging herself, and toppling the stereotypes that have threatened to pigeonhole the young women of Hollywood for decades.

One

GROOMED FOR THE STAGE

here is something about Neve Campbell that sets her apart from her glossy silver-screen counterparts like Natalie Portman and Liv Tyler. One need not strain to imagine her suffering a bad hair day or even an emotional crisis. For beneath the flawless hair and makeup lies a subtle, yet instantly recognizable, brand of grit. Her eyes speak volumes. One look and it's clear that this is one twenty-something who's had enough pain to last a lifetime. The sadness lurking beneath her gaze is, perhaps, the most potent contributor to her popularity with audiences nationwide. Neve is a real person, and she has quite a history to prove it.

The story begins on the actress's birthday, October 3, 1973, in Guelph, Ontario, Canada. No truly riveting account, however, is without its history. In Neve's case the plot is that of an acting dynasty, not unlike that of her contemporary and onetime costar, Drew Barrymore. While the names of Neve's grandparents may not have been of the household variety, like the legendary Barrymores, they too were actors who passed down their love of the craft to their offspring.

The Campbells were a solid, working-class family from Glasgow, Scotland. According to Neve, both of her "Scottish grandparents used to perform for soldiers during World War II." Although Neve's grandparents managed to put on brave faces for the men in uniform, the ravages of the war had induced their son to leave his beleaguered motherland behind for a better life in Canada. There he thought he would find equal opportunity instead of a rigid social order intent on enforcing the status quo. "Everything in Canada, we were told, was better than it was back in Scotland," Neve told the *Patriot Ledger*.

Such fervent patriotism indicates that Gerry Campbell did indeed find the golden fleece for which he'd made his trans-Atlantic voyage. The young man soon enrolled in the theater department of the University of Windsor, located at 401 Sunset Avenue in Windsor, Ontario, Canada. Acting was his sole aspiration, and the university provided him with numerous opportunities to flex his dramatic muscle in theatrical productions. It was also at university that Gerry met his future wife, Marnie Neve.

The two were brought together by a play in which they'd both won parts. Gerry took an immediate interest in this fetching brunette with delicate features. A first-generation Canadian, Marnie was of Dutch descent. Like her Scottish classmate, she too was following in her parents' footsteps by pursuing her passion for acting. Neve revealed to her fans that her "maternal grandparents were performers during and after the war—in Amsterdam, Holland." Since Marnie's parents had also immigrated to Canada, she completely understood Gerry Campbell's quest for artistic opportunity and creative freedom. A courtship was sparked, and nuptials ensued in 1970.

The couple chose to make their home in the Toronto suburb of Guelph, located about an hour's drive from the city. The newlyweds selected this area as much for its inexpensive housing costs as for its predominantly Scottish population. By the time their daughter was born in 1973, the marriage had already produced one son,

Christian, born on May 12, 1972, and a considerable amount of domestic turmoil. In honor of Marnie's lovely maiden name, which she was told meant "snow" in Spanish, the Campbells named their newborn Neve.

Even with the new baby's arrival, Gerry and Marnie couldn't seem to hold their family together. Soon the prospect of staying married for the sake of the children ceased to be tenable. The Campbells separated in 1976 when Neve was only three years of age.

An agreement between the parents left Neve living at the Campbells' old home in Guelph, sixty miles west of Toronto, with Marnie, while Christian stayed with Gerry, who lived in the Mississauga area of western Toronto. Shuffled back and forth between her mother and father, Neve had to endure her parents' disdain for one another. Since both were still in their late twenties, they each began dating again. The stream of people flowing in and out of Neve's life left the youngster bewildered about her role in the world, and lacking a secure family framework from which to build her own budding identity.

In addition, the immigrant mentality did little to make her life any easier. "My father's from lower-class Glasgow and my grandparents went through very difficult times during the war," she explained to TNT's *Rough Cut* Web site on cable television. "They had a lot of struggles, and it wasn't really okay to complain."

Neve took refuge in the world of make-believe. Considering her parents' vocations, the feat was anything but Herculean. Gerry taught high school drama and directed an amateur Scottish theater troupe in his spare time; Marnie was the enterprising young owner of a dinner theater. Simply watching her parents perform their daily responsibilities was an exercise in escapism. It facilitated Neve's immersion in a vivid imaginary world.

As far back as Campbell can remember, the aura of creative expression permeated every nook and cranny of her household. She had, in fact, been performing since she first learned to walk. In an interview with *Sassy* magazine, her brother Christian recalled, "our lives were centered around performing." He also spoke of a telling "picture of Neve and me, and she's in diapers and we're dancing for our parents in the living room. That's the way I was raised."

Neve's parents made sure to equip their children with a solid cultural education. Music, art, and, of course, theater played a large role in the young girl's early development. Constantly surrounded by thespians, Neve never imagined an existence other than that of becoming a performer. As she would tell *Twist* magazine, "My entire family is involved in the arts somehow. I've never assumed that I'd be anything but a performer."

The odds of Neve finding a future on the stage were increased by her parents' well-meaning encouragement. Sensing that their children showed a real proclivity for the arts, they encouraged both Neve and Christian's burgeoning talents. The Campbells harbored no ill feelings toward the acting vocation. While they may not have broken through as "stars" themselves both had been able to capitalize on their talent.

Three-year-old Neve was a constant presence at her mother's dinner theater. She'd sit at a table and watch the actors running their lines, transfixed by the dynamics she saw unfolding on the small stage. When show time would roll around at last, she'd have already seen the play in its entirety. Retreating to the back of the room, she would find a whole new spectacle at which to wonder— the patrons' reactions to the actors and the play.

Immersed in the world of performing arts since birth, Neve's destiny was all but decided. The latest in a long lineage of performers, both nature and nurture conspired to turn the young girl into an aspiring actress. By the age of four, the little girl was already imagining her name on a marquee.

At the tender age of four, Neve's life was turned upside down once again. Accustomed to living with her mother and visiting her father, she suddenly found this familiar arrangement reversed. She and her belongings were packed up and sent sixty miles to her father's neck of the woods—Mississauga, in the western section of Toronto. This major relocation and first-time separation from her mother was a traumatic experience for the little girl. Living with her father provided a study in contrasts. Neve had to adjust to a completely foreign set of circumstances, learning a great deal in the confusing process.

Fortunately, life with her dad was also replete with its own share of diversions. On countless occasions, Neve and Christian would tag along with Gerry to watch him direct his local theater group. Observing the actors rehearse, the children came to think that performing and adulthood went hand in hand. When they grew up, each thought, they, too, would be able to play pretend with the grownups.

In a happy turn of events, neither sibling would have to wait to come of age in order to experience the wonderful thrills of applause. As soon as Gerry felt that they knew how to conduct themselves accordingly, he had his youngsters assume the children's roles in his amateur productions. "I made my first appearance on stage at five," Neve informed the *Tennessean*, "as one of the children in *Aladdin and His Magic Lamp*."

Neve's theatrical education was by no means a formal one. While she may have assisted her dad whenever a play required a young girl's presence onstage, Gerry never instructed his children in the techniques of stage acting. He "never actually taught my older brother, Christian, and me how to act," Neve told the *Mr.*

Showbiz Web site. "It was just sort of observing and watching him, and growing up in the amateur theatre group in Toronto that we performed with when we were kids, which my father directed. It was really just observing the direction he gave to other people."

Despite Gerry's hands-off approach to his children's technical education, he was by no means a lax parent. Whereas Marnie had been nurturing, Gerry was exacting. When he first noticed his children's interest in acting, he began pressuring them to excel. "My father really believed in my brother and me," Neve said in an interview with *US* magazine. "Sometimes it was hard because he pushed us."

Under their father's circumspect gaze, Neve and Christian were steered even closer toward the arts. They remained as fascinated by the creative process as ever, and Neve recalled having "a blast doing pantomime and theater." Had their background been any different, the youngsters may have been considered far too young to be serious. Yet with each parent, and their respective coteries, in fervent pursuit of creative fulfillment via the stage, the chances of either sibling abandoning the dream of performing were becoming slimmer by the day.

Born only eighteen months apart, Neve and her brother were constant companions. Their common interest in theater only served to further bind the already close-knit siblings. The stoic nature of her adult relatives ensured that some of Neve's most carefree times were spent in play with her brother. As is often the case in first-generation immigrant families, the children's place is to be seen and not heard. "If there was anger, it was held in because it wasn't allowed to come out," Neve said on TNT's *Rough Cut* Web site. "I think that's why I love acting and why I dance, because I didn't really feel free to express my emotions as a child."

From the very beginning, Neve had demonstrated all the markings of a serious child. "My mother says that on the day I was born, she looked in my eyes and said I was one day old going on thirty," Neve confided to the *Buffalo News*. "I guess I'm what is called an old soul." The sentiment has been echoed by her costars of recent years, such as Scott Wolf of *Party of Five*, and by other members of the Campbell clan. "The catch phrase was 'Neve—fifteen going on forty,'" Christian told *US* magazine.

The family dynamic certainly did not discourage the development of Campbell's more thoughtful and sedate faculties. Having been brought up on stories of her Scottish grandparents' innumerable tribulations, Neve felt doubly pressured to keep her feelings to herself. "You always knew when she was pissed off—this sullen darkness would come over her face. She wouldn't complain, but you knew she was upset," Christian explained to *Rolling Stone*. "That's her strength: She holds it all in, holds it close to the chest. At the same time, that's her weakness. It makes her sort of hard to get to. You wonder what's going on in there."

Christian was, and continues to be, a veritable authority on his sister. Shared goals and obstacles ensured that the duo would rarely find cause to argue. "We're very similar," Neve told *Australian Hits*. "My brother and I are both very focused and we always have been, and determined. My brother's a wonderful, wonderful person. He's probably my best friend in the whole world and we're extremely close."

Life wasn't all about practice-makes-perfect for the two preschoolers. Like millions of other kids their age, Neve and Christian found ample opportunity to watch TV, setting their alarm clocks by Saturday morning cartoons. For obvious reasons, the pair related mostly to The Wonder Twins. "They were awesome," Neve enthused to *Genre* magazine. "They were always together and their power's together."

Neve's emphasis on togetherness is not the least bit surprising considering the void that her parents' separation had left in her young life. Their divorce had been bad enough; being uprooted again at age four imbued the child with a profound sadness. Her parents' second marriages only served to further depress her. "I was very insecure," Neve admitted. "I think a large part of it was because I didn't have a totally stable home life and I had to mature very quickly."

Growing up fast was not easy. "When you don't have a real solid family grounding, you kind of have to take care of yourself," she told *Rolling Stone*. Suffering the effects of domestic displacement and shifting parental figures, Neve was the consummate outsider, and she felt it. "I had a real hard time relating to people my age," she said. "I don't know, jokes just to be giddy didn't make a whole lot of sense to me."

Neve might have guessed that her school days were going to be a series of mini-tragedies from one of her early experiences on the playground. For months she'd been nursing a crush for young Sammy, the second grade's resident Lothario. Waging a heated competition on his affections against one Andrea, Neve would learn the hard way where her heartthrob's loyalties lay. "When I was seven we had this kissing contest and I wanted to kiss Sammy, but he was doing it with Andrea so I had to kiss Larry Hammond [another classmate]," Neve recounted to *FHM* magazine. "I kissed Larry and it only lasted about three seconds. I thought I was going to throw up afterwards, because he'd just eaten a peanut butter sandwich and it was all over the inside of his mouth."

While it all may have started out comically enough, the schooltime drama took a more serious turn as the years progressed. The birth of her father's sons, her half-siblings (Damian and Alex), had Neve feeling more put-upon than ever. Although she loved her little brothers dearly, the attention junkie in Neve yearned for the bygone days when she'd been the acknowledged baby in the family. With the entry of two younger children into the household, Neve was expected to assume an even more responsible role. Her new circumstances stacked yet another brick on the wall of social isolation, dividing Neve from her grade-school contemporaries. "It wasn't a horrible situation, but you're forced to grow up a little more quickly," Neve explained to *Soap Opera Digest*. "I usually don't even say that Alex and Damian are my half brothers," she was quick to add. "They're my whole brothers and I love them to death."

From the ages of seven to ten, Neve became "the biggest loser in school," she admitted to TV talk show host Rosie O'Donnell. "I was the kid who had to sit with the chaperones, or the matrons, at lunch, because no one would sit with me." It was a horrible time that no amount of success can ever efface from her memory. Each new day would add a fresh insult to the injury of being completely without friends. A particularly humiliating event occurred when she was nine years old: "We had this awful thing at school," she told *TV Guide*, "where we had cookies on Valentine's Day, and every student could buy them and send them to other class members. They would call up each student every time their name came out of the box. I was called up once because the teacher gave me a cookie. I was devastated. No one would spend five cents to send me a cookie."

Campbell's education was beset by a number of such soul-crushing incidents. For instance, there was the time when all the boys in her class banded together and wrote "a song that talked about how ugly I was," Neve told *FHM*. "It described each girl in my class, from the prettiest to the ugliest, and I was the last one. The end of the song just went: 'Neveurrggh, Neveurrggh,' like they were throwing up."

Anyone who's ever been singled out for schoolyard persecution, or sat through a screening of the sensitively-told film *Welcome to the Dollhouse* (1995), is likely to relate to the actress's poignant tale of childhood woe. For while the scared little girl still resides within the Neve that millions of viewers know and love, there was nothing of the self-assured starlet about her in those younger days. She was never so above it all that she could pretend that the slights didn't bother her. More than anything, she just wanted to be accepted. "Oh, I would try," she insisted. "Like any kid, desperately, every moment thinking, 'Oh, they smiled at me. Wait, maybe they do like me!'"

If there was one thing that Neve wanted even more than the convivial society of her peers, it was to become a prima ballerina. The dream was born when she was a first grader in 1979. As part of the informal cultural enrichment program that her parents had set in motion the day she was born, Neve was exposed to every form of fine art imaginable. Nothing, however, had ever moved her like her first visit to the ballet. "My father took me to see *The Nutcracker* when I was six," Neve told *US*. From that day hence, she says, becoming a ballet dancer "became my dream."

For Neve, acting no longer held the same creative allure. Thoughts of the grace and beauty of ballerinas, not to mention their billowy white skirts, filled the young girl's head. Like countless little girls before her, Neve insisted that she be enrolled in dance classes immediately after seeing *The Nutcracker*. Soon enough she had her way.

In a recent interview, Christian Campbell remarked that his sister always had a "determined look on her face." The hard-set jaw and intense gaze that have become famous the world over have always been part of Neve's aspect. More than distinctive physical attributes, the features were definite signs of the girl's strong character and resolve. Neve proved her mettle in dance class, where her innate sense of movement and musicality helped her capture the active enthusiasm of her teachers.

Neve's natural abilities, coupled with her love for the ballet, saw her progress faster than anyone could have anticipated. In dance she found the great release she'd unconsciously been seeking. While Campbell may have felt pressured to remain on her best behavior at home, in the dance studio she felt free to let loose. All the repressed anger and frustration she had toward her divorced parents and her cruel classmates was channeled into her dancing and before long she'd all but surpassed her teachers. Executing the intricate ballet moves to her instructors' satisfaction provided Campbell with some of her happiest moments. Finally, she had found the secret to feeling confident, talented, and beautiful. Neve was in her element.

As the pastime evolved into an all-consuming passion, Neve began to withdraw even further from the world of childish play. More and more, she would turn to the studio in search of her center and her true self. Once her parents, Marnie and Gerry, noticed her marked improvement, they joined her teachers in urging the youngster to excel. Plans of greatness took shape in their minds. It looked as though Neve could really go all the way professionally.

In all of Canada, there was only one institution that could bring a ballet dancer to the very zenith of success—the National Ballet School of Canada. Located at 105 Maitland Street in Toronto, Ontario, the company's headquarters are situated within an imposing nineteenth-century mansion. The school's name was pronounced with the utmost reverence in every local dance class, as its admissions personnel held the future careers of the country's young hopefuls in their hands. Every year the National Ballet School's talent scouts canvassed the country's dance studios in search of candidates for the new class.

The competition was so steep that it was that rare dance student who could claim actually knowing someone who'd been admitted; most merely knew someone who knew someone. In effect, getting into the prestigious ballet school was nothing short of winning the Rhodes Scholarship for dance.

As soon as Neve was old enough to audition, her father, Gerry, saw to it that she did not miss out on the opportunity. To prepare for the momentous event, she trained harder than ever, pushing her nine-year-old body to its very limits of endurance. Bearing witness to his daughter's tremendous drive, Gerry felt somewhat helpless. He did what little he could, however, to advance her cause. "My dad bought me a pink leotard, and pink socks and shoes," she recalled years later in *Mademoiselle* magazine, "and when we got there, we found out there was an audition uniform: black leotard, white socks, and pink ballet slippers. So there I was, all in pink, and I didn't fit in."

Neve overcame her initial embarrassment. For the better part of the prior three years, she'd had one career goal in mind, and she was not going to let a pink leotard stand in the way of her success. As soon as the tryouts commenced, her determination took over. Neve completely forgot about her inappropriate attire and focused on the matter at hand. As she performed her pliés, pirouettes, and jetés, she could sense the talent scout's eyes following her every move. With each encouraging remark that came her way, she could feel her poise and confidence swell.

The audition over, Neve and thirty other contenders awaited the imminent verdict. Some of them had traveled great distances for the audition, and some—hoping to slim down their proportions—hadn't eaten for days. All participants had hinged their most febrile hopes and dreams upon the outcome of this key dance session. Of course, as the recruiter would inform the dancers, all of them couldn't possibly be granted admission. All save one—the girl in the pink leotard—would return home in a state of dejection.

Despite the assurance she felt while dancing, Neve could hardly believe that she'd made the initial cut. Out of some two thousand would-be National Ballet School students, only 150 were invited back to the month-long summer program held at the school's headquarters. Even though only fifty would be granted entry to the school, suddenly Neve's chances of success had vastly improved. The drive back to Mississauga was the happiest of her life. A ball of euphoric energy, she finally understood what the ecstasy of victory felt like.

Neve's actual admission into the institution had yet to be accomplished. Before investing in mass quantities of point shoes, she had to survive the month-long summer program. Thereafter, only a select few would be chosen to continue dancing with the renowned school. But she wasn't too worried. For Neve, a month of dance lent credence to the old "getting there is half the fun" aphorism.

Anxious to share the good news, Neve called a fellow dancer, only to learn one of life's harder lessons: Misery loves nothing so much as company. Her pal had also auditioned, but without success. The other girl might have gotten over her setback sooner had she not learned of Campbell's triumph. "When she didn't get in, she stopped talking to me," Neve told *Mademoiselle*. "That was the first friend I lost that way."

Unaware that her success at forging new friendships would soon be hampered by her achievements, Neve blissfully contemplated her brilliant future. When the time came for her to leave for the summer program, she was ready. Being away from home and surrounded by unfamiliar faces was, no doubt, taxing for the shy and introverted little girl. Since bridging the social gap between herself and the other kids didn't seem feasible, Neve threw herself whole-heartedly into her dancing. With only one objective in mind, the social problems that plagued her outside the dance studio seemed to disappear.

Campbell loved to perform, and the summer program gave her ample opportunity to put on a show. Since Neve's quest for the limelight had reached critical momentum by this time, she had no trouble catching her evaluators' interest. "I remember when I realized how important it was for her to be on-stage," her brother told *TV Guide*. Gerry Campbell had cast him in one of his high school plays, and Christian recalled that when he came into the living room to model his stage costume, "Neve broke into tears because she felt so left out. People want to wrap her up and take care of her. Maybe that's what an audience feels when they watch Neve—her vulnerability."

Fortunately, the ballet recruiters had been struck more by her determination then her frailty. They would surely have barred Neve from admission into the rigorous training program had she evinced any outward signs of weakness. Even as she showed her softer side at home, she would not give her instructors any cause to doubt her abilities. Not that there was ever any chance of Neve losing her cool in action. The adrenaline rush she derived from dancing was sufficient unto itself to elevate her leaps above those of the competition. On the dance floor, Neve was already a star.

This powerful stage presence was not lost on the ballet school staff. After a month of backbreaking "fun," the young ballerina was called into the head administrator's office. Unsure as to the purpose of this summons, Neve hoped that it might have something to do with her admission status. Come what may, at least she would no longer have to live in doubt. The verdict was indeed in, and Campbell could hardly contain her joy. When "the principal called me into her office to tell me that I was accepted . . . I had to pee so badly, I had to hold myself!" Neve said during a Prodigy Online Chat, only half joking.

Neve's parents had never been financially well off. Since illustrious private schools—including prestigious ballet academies—are not cheap, they applied for, and received, a need-based scholarship for their daughter from the National Ballet School of Canada.

After a festive celebration in Neve's honor, Gerry made arrangements for his daughter's future at the school. His first order of business was to find a new place to live, closer to the Toronto-based school where Neve would now be a resident student. In the flurry of packing that followed, all the little ballerina could think about was her new life ahead. How would her dancing rate in relation to the other students? Would she still get to see her mother every weekend? Would her peers like her? Exhilaration, anticipation, and fear merged as Campbell contemplated her life to come.

The five years that followed these initial weeks of unadulterated glee would leave an indelible mark on Neve's already bruised psyche. Coming in with only the highest expectations, she never could have predicted the fate that awaited her. A blur of dull pain punctuated by moments of acute suffering, her career at the National Ballet School would begin with taunts and social isolation and end in an outright emotional collapse five years later.

Two

A TIME TO DANCE

hat's been the most difficult time for you?" In 1996, a twenty-three-year-old Neve Campbell considered the probing question posed by the *Mr. Showbiz* Web site for all of one second before answering.

"Probably when I was at the National Ballet School of Canada from the ages of nine to fourteen," she replied without skipping a beat.

Right away, young Campbell knew she was going to have problems in her new environment. The students at this school weren't like the ones she'd barely managed to fit in with back in Mississauga. They were from well-to-do families, and Neve was the subsidized student. "I grew up poor," she told the *Calgary Sun*. "I lived in apartments all my life." While the realization of her economic disadvantage may have been some time in the dawning, its consequences were readily apparent from the start at the ballet school. Her clothes were ridiculed by her fellow students, and her hopes of belonging were abruptly dashed.

Prior to enrolling at the ballet school, Neve had never found much cause to worry about her socioeconomic status. Since she'd always been preoccupied by dance and her family difficulties, it took her a while to figure out why none of her peers seemed to like her. Physically, she was essentially no different from anybody else. "Everybody was pretty," she told *Rolling Stone*. "We were all being bred to be ballerinas. We all looked alike; our bodies looked alike."

Yet it was here that her social alienation began to take hold and fester. The Valentine's Day cookie incident, the disparaging song, and the solitary lunches were all milestones that took place after Neve's admission to the National Ballet School. In the span of one semester, her first at the school, her entire perspective shifted. Living in residence, she couldn't help but notice the many differences between herself and her classmates. Their designer clothes, exotic vacation destinations, and desirable home addresses all led the young dancer to one conclusion—the others looked down on her because they came from money and she did not.

Her self-consciousness over her relatively meager circumstances did little to buoy her social station. Neve was quickly branded a loser. With a sum total of fourteen students in her class, finding a fellow scapegoat with whom to commiserate was impossible. That whole first year of school could accurately be described as Neve against the ballet school's entire fifth grade—a class struggle by any definition.

The damage sustained by her young psyche during these crucial formative years cannot be overestimated. In non–work related situations, Neve still tends to shy away from crowds. The consequences of childhood trauma are such that the actress must brace herself every time she is thrust into the spotlight. Having had to inure herself against censure so often as a young girl, she must now struggle to express the full gamut of her emotions. "I didn't cry a whole lot as a kid," she once explained. "I still don't. Sometimes I'll go through things, and my friends will be like, 'Neve, why aren't you reacting to this?' I try to watch myself."

Unpopular youngsters often fall into one of two categories; they either push themselves to succeed to make up for what is lacking in their social lives, or they grow so depressed and withdrawn that nothing can save them from falling prey to the underachiever's vicious cycle. The coping skills Neve acquired while dealing with her parents' broken marriage—repressing her feelings and wearing a courageous façade—helped her take the high road at school. By now she was an old hand at compartmentalizing the disparate realms of her complex life.

While she may have been the butt of prepubescent humor on the social front, she would have her revenge in the dance studio. Training in six types of dance, and spending anywhere from three to five hours a day, six days a week in dance class gave the chronic outsider ample opportunity to outshine, outdo, and outdance her tormentors. Their mean-spirited raillery only spurred her on. Every derisive comment, every sneer, and every peal of laughter at her expense fanned the flames of her ambition.

Knowing little of her personal tribulations, the school's instructors were struck by her determination and ability. "She was always very focused and hardworking," recalled Mavis Staines, the school's artistic director since 1989, in *Seventeen* magazine. "She was someone who, both in the studio and on stage, I was just drawn to. That is part of what talent is all about. She really has it in spades."

Neve was chosen from among her classmates to join the corps in that year's production of *The Nutcracker*. Only three years had passed since the night she'd sat in a darkened auditorium watching the National Ballet of Canada perform the first ballet production she had ever seen. Knowing that she would now be the one on stage, perhaps inspiring other little girls to take to the dance barre, was a handsome reward that made many of her problems seem small in comparison. This boost strengthened her resolve to withstand her peers' stiff opposition. "I wanted to be there because I wanted to be a dancer," she explained to the *Mr. Showbiz* Web site. "I love to dance, and that was my dream. When you're in that school, it means you've beaten out two thousand people to get there, so you're not exactly gonna quit."

To rehearse for the performance, Campbell was required to spend even more hours dancing. Thus, winning the part was more than a simple honor, but a saving grace. The less time she would have to spend with her contemporaries the better. As she concentrated all of her energy on perfecting the complex maneuvers, the hours of practice flew by. At rehearsal's end each day, it was with a dejected heart that Neve would make her way back to the dormitory or cafeteria to confront her peers.

Nowhere was the contrast between her lowly position in the school pecking order and the mastery she'd achieved over her art more jarring than in performance. The usually unassuming schoolgirl, mocked as the ugliest in her class, never failed to transform into a swan on stage. Considering the self-esteem–damaging circumstances in which she was embroiled, those who didn't know the eleven-year-old Neve may have found her near total lack of stage fright astounding. The confidence she displayed before an audience was no small indication that performing, as she's now told many an interviewer, was truly in her blood.

The Nutcracker wasn't the last of Neve's school-day glories. Having proven her competence, she would be called to dance with the company yet again in a production of *Sleeping Beauty*. She would never forget the sheer thrill of these performances, telling the *Australian Star*, "I've danced in productions of *Sleeping Beauty* and *The Nutcracker* in Canada that I think were my 'height' as a dancer."

The special attention bestowed upon Neve by the school's staff didn't earn her any points with her fellow dancers. If anything, her talent was the bane of her classmates' daily lives. The dog-eat-dog atmosphere fostered by the ballet school made certain of that. All the students in the program had the same goal. As she told TNT's *Rough Cut* Web site, "From fifth to thirteenth grade, all you ever aspire to do is get into the company. There's a real backstabbing mentality to the school."

When Neve was handpicked to appear in *The Nutcracker*, she incurred the other students' full envy. Located in Toronto, the National Ballet of Canada is one of the world's leading international dance companies, with more than forty-five professional dancers and a symphony orchestra. "The competition was terrific," Neve revealed to the *Patriot Ledger*. "In my class of fourteen, it was known that only two could make it into the company." As one's success meant the others' failure, the dance students' dislike of Neve quickly turned into outright contempt. Living in residence without a shoulder to cry on, the nine-year-old developed a tough skin. Surrounded by adversaries day and night, Neve learned how to deal with negative energy and to protect herself from her unpleasant rivals.

The thought of quitting was abhorrent to Neve and to all the other dancers at the National Ballet School. Every year that a dancer completed in the program was a triumph in and of itself. People did not drop out; they were dismissed. To keep the performers on their mark, the school made it clear that a student's tenure at the program could end at any given time. To Campbell that was "a lot of pressure," as she said to *USA Today* in 1997. "Every year, you're told whether you're going to be kicked out."

While she still loved to dance, Neve began to grow disgusted with the cutthroat world of ballet. In their quest for the stage, the dancers-in-training stopped at nothing to insinuate themselves into their instructors' good graces. The teachers often played along, picking favorites in order to spur on the rivalry and motivate their classes. Such tactics further distressed the already pressured teenagers, most of whom felt that life without dance was not worth living. As the years passed, Neve would reflect more and more upon the mind-set of her chosen profession. "I couldn't relate to the dance mentality," she confided to the *Journal Arts*. "I cannot relate to not eating, to the back-stabbing, to doing something that will keep you in pain. You could be in the corps de ballet the entire time, know the same thirty people for the rest of your career."

Since Neve was isolated from her classmates, years would pass before she realized that others at the school shared her qualms. In the meantime, she repressed her rebellious spirit, allowing only hints of her discontent to seep out. First, she decided to thwart the dress code by wearing her dad's leather jacket. When this minor transgression went unnoticed, Neve stepped up her mutinous efforts. One of the school's rules required that all ballerinas must keep their hair below shoulder-length, in order to fit it into a conventional bun come dance time. On an impulse Campbell dared to subvert the edict. "I was really upset with the school," she told *FHM* magazine, "and I went and had the back of my head shaved, so that when I had my hair up, the bun sat on the back of a bald head. They were not happy with me at all. I would've been kicked out for anything more than that."

Naturally, the school also had its share of benefits. The strict code of conduct, for instance, was of great help to Campbell in one respect. As each dancer's entire existence was controlled by the National Ballet School's iron-fisted policy, there would be no staying home sick, no daydreaming in class, in short, no yielding to weakness of any kind. Neve absorbed a valuable lesson from the rigorous routine, acquiring an aversion to anything that might damage her physical well-being. Later in life, after reinventing herself as an actress, Neve would credit the school with allowing her to "remain stable in this business, both psychologically and physically. It wasn't just the discipline, it was understanding the need to take care of yourself and realizing that if you want to be successful you must be prepared to do the work."

Well aware of the extraordinary demands they made of their students, the school staff went to great lengths to counteract the potential hazards of their rigid educational style—hiring seven therapists to service a mere 125 students. Each student could expect to receive the type of personal attention unheard of at a public school. "I mean, they're wonderful and try to take care of you," Neve said of the administration, "but they have many, many psychologists on staff so that kind of tells you something about it."

In the *Ottawa Citizen*, she attributed the school's handle-with-care approach to the fact that, in her opinion, "the most messed-up people sometimes come out of there." For a while Campbell seemed to be just one such messed-up individual herself.

In her five years at the school, Neve had not made a single friend. She never got used to the loneliness. "I got to a place at that school where I hated dance," she later admitted to *TV Guide*, "and that was really tragic for me. I had no friends, I didn't fit in, and I was living in residence. When you live with the people you don't fit in with, you're in trouble."

She sought out the sympathetic ear of her designated counselor. In her therapy sessions, Neve revealed her hidden feelings of dissatisfaction with the school. The psychological strain of the constant career pressures, her repugnance with the ballet dancer's requisite mind-set, her dance-induced physical problems, and her disenchantment with dance in general were discussed and documented in a classified file. Yet talking through her problems was not enough to revive Neve's flagging motivation. "I'd just about given up on my dream of being a dancer," she told the *Mr. Showbiz* Web site.

Finally, she could take it no longer. Whether or not she remained at the school, a future in dance seemed untenable to her. Having planned to dance her entire life, however, Neve did not know what to do. Thanks to the National Ballet School's exacting training schedule and pressure-cooker environment, fourteen-year-old Neve was already suffering from arthritis, hip problems, and a badly bruised self-image. Still, to quit was something else altogether.

One doesn't simply let go of their life's work without a fight, especially not if that someone is as strong-willed as Neve Campbell. Her sense of self was so inextricably bound to dance that she could not conceive of an existence devoid of her childhood dream. Who was she if not a dancer? The thought of forsaking her plans threw Neve into a state of chaotic confusion. As she told *USA Today*, "I pretty much had a nervous breakdown at fourteen."

When Neve's psychologist chose to divulge the contents of her personal file to the school's director, Neve saw the betrayal as just another reason to quit the ballet world. In truth, she no longer felt as if she had any choice in the matter. The emotional collapse she'd suffered was so obviously the result of her mind, body, and soul rising up in protest against the National Ballet School's toxic atmosphere that Neve realized she would no longer be "able to function" if she did try to stick it out.

Neve's sudden departure shook the entire school, and gave her peers, as well as her former instructors, plenty to talk about. One day she would come to realize that even this dark phase occurred for a reason. In fact it was probably the best thing that could have happened to her. Now when she stops to consider what might have been had she stayed, she can only shake her head and say, "I like myself too much."

After Neve's disastrous defection from the National Ballet School of Canada in 1987, she accepted that being a prima ballerina was not in her future. "When I quit," she told *Sassy*, "I thought I would never dance again." While it may have taken a breakdown to pound the last nail into the coffin of Neve's dance aspirations, she was at last free to lead her life the way she saw fit. Her narrow escape from an existence to which she was ill suited presented the fourteen-year-old with a wealth of new options and opportunities. She'd missed a lot of living being confined to that school. Her greatest hope now was to make up for lost time.

The real world beckoned, and Neve wanted nothing so much as to drink from the fountain of normal life. After a short period of regrouping, she enrolled in public high school. Despite her pretty face, sweet disposition, and whip-smart intelligence, she once again found herself cast in the role of loner. Years of standing on the outside looking in had left her ill equipped to make meaningful connections with her peers.

At least at her new school, Neve had the freedom to fade into the background. Since the number of students in her tenth grade class was well over one hundred, Neve could blend in with her classmates. She made no waves and applied herself to her studies. Though her life was simple and peaceful, Neve was *not* happy. She'd become accustomed to a certain amount of strife, and yearned to strive toward a goal as she had in the old days.

Living once again with her father—who had already remarried and divorced again—Neve had plenty of time to share in the family fold. She loved spending time with her older brother, who was now studying acting at Toronto's prestigious Claude Watson School for the Arts. Talking to Christian about his experiences soon convinced Neve to follow in his footsteps. Recalling all the fun she'd had acting as a youngster, she chose consorting with her brother and pursuing a performing arts education over being lonely and uninspired at a regular educational facility.

The Claude Watson School was the ideal locale for a young girl who'd endured five years of being "treated like a child" in ballet class. The school catered to professional students. The many artists, actors, singers, and athletes who attended had their pick of courses and could schedule their hours around their professional endeavors. Although nothing in her past had prepared Neve for this kind of freedom, she was mature enough to handle it without getting carried away. "In Canada, kids are exposed to different things," Campbell explained. "Like school is very different; it's not nearly as social. Canadian teenagers see it as a much more serious place."

A self-confessed "geek," Christian's popularity also left much to be desired, and he was glad to have Neve in his corner. Although fraternizing with her brother was not Neve's ticket to the whirlwind life of boyfriends and parties, his constant presence lifted her spirits considerably. Most likely, it was this special relationship between the siblings that convinced her parents to let her transfer out of public high school and into the considerably more expensive alternative school. Neve's renewed interest in performing pleased Marnie and Gerry, and they gave her their unconditional support. It had taken some time, but Neve was her old self again.

Six months after she'd bid farewell to her dancing shoes, Neve was already attending her second high school. This fast pace was not destined to decelerate at Claude Watson. She had only been at the school a short while when Hal Prince arrived in Toronto to stage a production of Andrew Lloyd Webber's *Phantom of the Opera*. As the Tony Award–winning director and producer of such renowned musicals as *Fiddler on the Roof*, *West Side Story*, and *Evita*, Prince had been a major force in theater for decades. He was greeted with a great deal of fanfare by the city's artistic community. Everyone in creative circles was talking about the auditions for *Phantom*, and as a performing arts school student, Neve heard as much about the auditions as anyone.

When Campbell first contemplated trying out for the show, she was hesitant. After all, she had just recently closed the chapter on her dreams of dance. Luckily, the magical pull of the stage won out in the nick of time. She decided to give the footlights a try, if only for the experience. Completely cognizant of the great mass of dancers who would be vying for the same handful of positions, Neve understood that the odds of prevailing were stacked against her. Yet she had never tried out for a professional role before, and curiosity got the best of her.

The day of the audition found Neve jittery and unsure. When she arrived at the designated spot, the sight of all those trained dancers limbering up had her wanting to rush for the nearest exit. She made a beeline for the dressing room, planning to chalk the whole experience up to an error in judgment. "There were like 300 girls at this cattle-call audition," Neve recalled, "and I was so nervous, I was bawling my eyes out."

When a few compassionate hopefuls noticed Neve's distress, they rushed to her side. She rallied after her fellow dancers' pep talk, and proceeded to face the judges. The applicants were called onstage in groups of twelve, and she patiently awaited her turn. Now that she'd seen what these cattle calls were all about, the only thing left to do was put her best foot forward. The process could only get easier from here. A voice roused her from her reveries.

"Nevay Camembera," it called.

Neve briefly surveyed the room. Since no one else responded to the announcer's call, she got up to take her place on stage. This was by far the worst mispronunciation of her name she'd ever encountered. While few people had ever garbled her surname of Campbell, many over the years had failed to enunciate her first name correctly. *Nev*-ie, *Nev*-ay, Neeve, she'd heard them all, but Nevay Camembera, as she told *TV Guide*, was by far the most bewildering. "All of a sudden I was a cheese."

The mispronunciation of her name, however, would have to go unremarked, as she had more important matters to deal with now. *Here goes*, she thought, as she ran to the stage. Although the dance combinations required for the audition were by no means a stretch for the former ballerina, she knew that the other young women were professional dancers, with years of experience. Once in the spotlight, though, Neve's worries gave way to her immense focus, and all of her nervous energy was channeled into executing the routine properly. The choreographer picked her out of the group instantly.

She was called back again and again, until finally there were only twelve candidates left in the running, "... and I was one of them," she recalled in a *USA Today* interview. When this last group was informed that they had the stage jobs, Neve could hardly believe it. She had figured that her inexperience would work against her. Expecting to come away enriched only for the experience, Neve was not mentally prepared for the job offer.

In a flash life as she knew it was over. As one of *Phantom's* new Degas Girls (a chorus line of female dancers) she'd be required to perform daily and would be paid handsomely for her efforts. Better still, she could look forward to learning the ins and outs of show business and rest easy in the knowledge that she was no longer on the outside looking in. This was the kind of break for which many stage performers wait all their lives. And here she was, a paid professional with a prestigious production at just fifteen years of age.

Neve wasn't the only one shocked by the day's events. When the director found out that one of the members of their ballet chorus line was still in her early teens, he was dumbfounded. "It was a pretty good feeling," Neve told *TV Guide*, "The choreographer said, 'How old are you, dear?' When I said fifteen, she couldn't believe it, and Hal Prince was going, 'Oh, my God! She's fifteen!' The next youngest dancer was twenty-four. I was the youngest to do *Phantom* anywhere in the world." The producers had a hard time believing that she could keep pace with the exacting work schedule, but their fears were laid to rest when they learned of her training at the National Ballet School of Canada, and her enrollment at one of Toronto's most respected schools for professional teens.

So began the happiest period in Neve's life. The joy she found in her work was all the more acute for its sharp contrast to her days as a ballet student. Received with open arms by her older peers, she went from being an outcast to being everybody's favorite. As the resident little sister, she was lavished with the kind of attention she hadn't enjoyed since early childhood. "I still think of that as the best experience of my life," she recently told *Cosmopolitan* magazine. "I was so young and extremely enthusiastic. Everyone in the cast was older—and they all looked after me and showed me the ropes."

Learning the ropes involved more than executing the relatively simple dance steps required of the chorus. As the understudy for the principal role of Meg, Neve had to learn musical theater acting. In addition to vocal training, she had to memorize dialogue and learn to emote to a full auditorium by magnifying her slightest gestures for the benefit of the audience. Anyone wondering today where Neve Campbell picked up her attention to the details of dramatic expression need look no further than her *Phantom* days.

The rarefied world of professional acting proffered other benefits as well. As if learning valuable skills, upgrading her résumé, and working with giants such as Hal Prince was not enough, Campbell was also well remunerated for the privilege. The fact that she was making more money than her parents was hard to fathom, but even more ironic was the fact that her earning power eclipsed even that of the principals dancing with the National Ballet of Canada. "I was one of the highest-paid professional dancers in Canada," she told *Journal Arts*, "making as much as the stars of the National Ballet. That's really sad."

Neve's newfound career and financial independence were bound to affect her lifestyle sooner or later. She took charge of her affairs right away. With the support of her parents, she opted to forgo her high school education in order to fully devote herself to her career. "It was my parents' dream for themselves, but they married young and had my brother Christian and I right away so they couldn't pursue professional acting careers," she confided to the *Calgary Sun*. "They're living their dreams through us and have been our greatest supporters and fans."

Although she would one day wonder about all that she'd missed in her youth, dropping out of tenth grade made perfect sense to Neve at the time. As she explained to *TV Guide*, "All of a sudden I'm fifteen, and the member of a fantastic company. So it didn't make a lot of sense to say, 'Oh, I'm not going to take *The Phantom of the Opera* because I need to learn more about history.'"

Neve's interest had never been piqued by schoolbooks. She had dreamt of nothing but performing her whole life. Having enrolled at the National Ballet School in fifth grade, when most school children have yet to discover their favorite subjects, she had grown used to relegating academics to the background. Math, science, and the like were only so many obstacles to overcome in her quest for the stage. Now that she was financially secure and accepted as an adult in the artistic community, she saw no reason to carry on the facade of thirsting for knowledge, when all she truly yearned for was the spotlight.

The feisty teen's next logical move would take her out from under her father's roof. If any sixteen-year-old can ever really be ready for such complete autonomy, Neve was. Unlike many of her contemporaries, who spent years dodging parental curfews, she had been responsible for herself since her entry into the realm of serious ballet. Even her parents' marital foibles served to endow her with a strong survival instinct. Feeling ages older than her sixteen years, she mustered up the courage to inform her father of her imminent relocation. "I was doing *Phantom*," she told *Mademoiselle*, "working with people who were my father's age and older, and being treated on an equal basis with them. You grow up very quickly, and it doesn't make sense to [answer to] someone whom you could consider a peer."

Neve's parents couldn't have been too worried about her safety. Since she planned to move in with her older brother, Christian, who'd set the precedent for leaving the family home prematurely, they could rest assured that their little girl was in good hands. "Neve and I could always depend on having each other," Christian later told *Rolling Stone*.

The siblings' solid ties were the result of their uncertain familial terrain. After their parents divorced, each had remarried and divorced again. The Campbell's strained home life, which must have given rise to the rash of divorces, was also the impetus for Neve and her brother's early withdrawal from their family. In *Rolling Stone*, Christian made a point of declaring that his "family is amazing. It's just discombobulated."

The relocation dropped the curtain on Neve's childhood and adolescence. As early as 1989, the sixteen-year-old was already a professional dancer and actress, as well as a self-sufficient career woman. After what seemed like a century of struggle, Neve Campbell was coming into her own at last.

Three

SHEDDING HER SKIN

he production of *Phantom of the Opera* in Toronto's pricey Pantages Theatre (located at 244 Victoria Street) in the summer of 1989, marked the beginning of Neve's emergence as the strong, confident, and charismatic young woman that she is today. Surrounded by a supportive and nurturing cast, Neve easily adapted to the grueling schedule. While many of her castmates rightly complained of the long hours and ceaseless performances, Campbell was quickly becoming addicted to the rush of being onstage. The theater was not simply about getting paid or doing her job. For Neve, the stage held a promise that her personal life had failed to offer—a pledge of transformation and unconditional acceptance.

During her five years at the National Ballet School of Canada, Neve had lived for the rare opportunity to showcase her talents, but in *Phantom* she finally got to experience that thrill on a daily basis. A consummate performer with an infinite capacity to sublimate her feelings for the good of the show, Campbell was beginning to feel the therapeutic benefits of donning her own mask on stage. The nightly performances changed her outlook toward the world and her place in it. Since she was spending more time on stage than off, the line between her shy former self and her self-assured onstage persona was becoming hazier with every pirouette. The illusion had finally become the reality, as Neve relinquished the mask she had unwillingly worn her entire life.

The Toronto-based production of *Phantom of the Opera* was met with rave reviews from audiences and critics alike. Heather Bird of the *Ottawa Sun* pronounced, "If you're paying good money to be dazzled, to be entertained and to enjoy, you've come to the right place. The audience rewarded the cast with frequent applause and a lengthy standing ovation. A smash hit!" Stephen Godfrey of the *Globe and Mail* also hailed the musical spectacle, calling it, "as spectacular and lavish as any grand opera and as colorful as the Cirque du Soleil. Director Harold Prince orchestrates the flow of scenes for this musical megahit with brilliant cinematic precision."

From an artistic standpoint, Campbell had never been so on top of her game. She was developing skills she didn't even know she had, including singing and acting. Her commitment to the arts was never so apparent than in her two-year tenure with the production. As a member of the show's ballet chorus, Neve's responsibilities were limited to showing up on time for rehearsals, stretching with the rest of the dancers before the performances, and turning in early for a good night's sleep. Fulfilling those obligations would have been enough had she only wanted to pursue a life in dance. Seeing the accolades and adoration given to the lead actors, however, ignited a new urge that grew into an all-consuming passion.

Neve was seized by a sudden desire to learn everything there was about the theater and she went out of her way to seek the counsel of her fellow performers and coaches. Instead of shunning the newcomer for her inexperience or her ill-concealed zealousness, the cast of *Phantom* took the young performer under its wing and aided her in her quest to find a dramatic voice. As she explained later to her fan club, "There I learned a tremendous amount about acting—and they trained my voice as well."

For the first time in her life, Neve was the darling of the group. Basking in the glow of her newfound popularity, Neve came to realize that her ambition was consuming her teenage years. "I go through times when I think, 'Wow, it would have been nice to have a normal childhood and not be dancing six hours a day,'" she revealed to *In the Mix* magazine.

The assertiveness she gained at the Pantages Theatre soon spilled over into her personal life. "The way my career has gone has given me confidence," she explained to *Mademoiselle*. "If I'd failed more, I might not be so confident." For the first time, she developed an interest in what other good things life had to offer. Although dating had never been a priority for the artistic-minded dancer, Neve, like most young girls her age, had fantasized about falling in love. This natural yearning, coupled with the burgeoning confidence she gained through *Phantom*, propelled Neve to seek out a partner who could show her what she had been missing all along.

Until this point in her life, Neve's encounters of the romantic kind had been what most people would describe as "disastrous." While the majority of first dates often fail to live up to expectations, her first dinner date only served to confirm her inexperience and naiveté. "I thought, 'I'm going to be dainty and order the soup,'" she told *Twist*. "I'd never had French onion soup before and I didn't realize that it was going to be impossible to eat. I thought it'd be a really classy thing to order. I tried desperately to pretend I was cool with it, but my date was just staring at me, like, 'What's the matter with you?' And of course, French onion soup isn't great for your breath. I have no idea what I was thinking."

Over the years Campbell had learned the ins and outs of dating etiquette, but she could never bring herself to play the role of the demure girl next-door. Meeting someone special had become important to Neve, but so was keeping her identity intact. Unlike her peers, who were looking for the perfect boyfriend to take them to the movies or to the prom, Campbell was not out to just snag a man. On the contrary, the need for friendship and mutual understanding were her primary motivators.

Unfortunately, her forthright and outspoken approach intimidated many prospective suitors, but she pressed onward, believing that romance would eventually find her.

Neve worried that the emotional detachment she experienced during her adolescence contributed to her inability to sustain a relationship. She tried all the harder to open herself up to new experiences, and dated a variety of guys from every background. "I went out with a guy called Aaron when I was seventeen because he used to have a Mohawk [haircut]," she expressed to *FHM*. "I thought he was the coolest guy. But he left me after three weeks."

The day Neve finally met the man with whom she would spend the next five years of her life was by no means remarkable. After a performance of *Phantom* she stopped at the Pantages Theatre's bar to relax. Jeff Colt was the bartender on duty that evening, and he and Neve soon struck up a lively conversation. Unlike most of the lackadaisical guys Neve had dated, Jeff was driven to succeed in much the same way she was. A songwriter and actor in his own right, bartending at the Pantages Theatre was only a temporary arrangement for Jeff. As a performer, Colt had yet to earn his stripes. He, however, was only too happy to be working so close to the action.

When the twenty-five-year-old aspiring actor met Neve she was only seventeen. So young and already so accomplished! With most couples, respect follows closely on the heels of physical attraction. Yet when Jeff discovered how talented and determined this young woman was, he was instantly attracted to her. For her part, here was a real man who would not be intimidated by her ambitious goals. How could he be, when he had harbored similar professional dreams for as long as he could remember?

Living on her own, Neve didn't have to deal with the hassles of parental supervision dictating when and with whom she could go out. This freedom gave the new couple ample time to learn more about each other. What used to be Campbell's time off from work became synonymous with time spent with Colt. "It's kind of like when you put your hand under hot water and for an instant you can't tell whether it's actually hot or cold. Love is the same thing," she expressed during a *Detour* interview. "It's overwhelming," Neve continued. "Your life is turned upside down. All of a sudden everything that was important in your life is no longer important, and it's all about that one person."

Neve was more than willing to exchange her privacy for the companionship Jeff offered. The chemistry between the pair was electric. With his well-built physique, tall stature, warm eyes, and light brown hair, Jeff fulfilled all of Neve's physical requirements. Never before had she met someone so appealing, and with whom she was so compatible.

Getting swept away by the happiness of her new relationship wasn't entirely characteristic of Neve. Her parents' early divorce had planted a deep-seated suspicion of "eternal" love and similar notions. She was, however, having too good a time with Jeff to reflect on the past. With her career on track and the independence she always craved at her fingertips, she was just beginning to feel the surge of exhilaration that comes with total control of one's life. In some respects, Campbell was still a child, but in many others she was a self-sufficient woman who paid her own bills and set her own rules. It was around this time that Neve made her first major purchase, a green Volkswagen Cabriolet. According to the performer, "It was my reward to myself."

Neve also yearned to play the part of a homemaker. Since moving in with her brother, she missed the comfort of having someone look after her and vice versa. Tough and resilient on the outside, she still needed to feel protected and loved, and to share intimate moments with a trustworthy person. While Christian had filled that role for several years, meeting Jeff Colt gave Neve the opportunity to loosen all ties with the past. Feeling securely loved for the first time, Neve squelched the doubts that were planted by her parents' multiple divorces. In the wake of her professional and personal triumphs, a wave of optimism washed over the seventeen-year-old Campbell. She decided to face the future with confidence. And if that meant committing herself to Jeff and fulfilling his desire to move in together, then that was exactly what she would do.

Four

ON THE VERGE

ajor life changes are often met with some degree of resistance. As an artist, however, Neve had no qualms about relinquishing control and flowing with the tides of her destiny. In fact, variety, much like breathing, had become a necessity for her. From being chosen to study at the National Ballet School of Canada, to being handpicked by Hal Prince for *Phantom*, Neve's professional course seemed guided by an unseen, powerful force. With so many things now falling into place—her relationship with Jeff Colt, her new life at the theatre—Neve renewed her faith in the universal plan; a faith that had been shattered in her tortured adolescence at the hands of her peers. No longer the victim of contrary circumstances, Campbell was eager to navigate the future, with all its unexpected twists and turns.

As soon as she and Jeff moved into a small apartment in Toronto, Neve had the kind of lucky break most young performers would go to great lengths to get. While performing in *Phantom*, she was spotted by a modeling agent in the audience.

When the talent representative approached Neve about entering the glamorous world of modeling, she was more than interested in the opportunity. The chance to make big money for a few hours of posing seemed like a cakewalk in comparison to the exhausting performance conditions under which she had been laboring for two years. With little hesitation, Neve accepted the offer and prepared to embark upon the new adventure.

Modeling, however, was not to be her final calling so much as a stepping stone in her labyrinthine voyage to success. Playing the role of an animated mannequin was by no means what she had expected. Having grown accustomed to exercising her creative muscles, Neve was bored by her new profession. Standing under hot lights for what seemed like an eternity with makeup artists and hairstylists hovering around like so many birds of prey, began to grate on her. "So I modeled for two months and hated it, only because I had trained professionally for years and years, and it didn't make sense to be just standing in front of a camera with everything being based on my looks," she griped to the *Mr. Showbiz* Web site in 1997.

The desire to make funny faces at the photographer and express herself through movement were, of course, strictly verboten in her new work. Also prohibited was the all-too-human impulse to speak her mind. Girls of lesser capabilities may have been thrilled to be in the spotlight. Neve, however, felt that her talents were being squandered for a mere paycheck.

Neve put up with the dehumanizing job for as long as she could. She would, however, put an end to her new career sooner than she had anticipated. Besides the malaise that comes with having to suck in one's cheekbones for a living, Campbell was also disgruntled with the exploitation common to the modeling industry. "I did a photo shoot for Sony, and I was in a bathing suit or something like that," Neve recalled to *Detour* magazine in March of 1998. "It was only supposed to be in the catalogue, and all of a sudden there was this huge, huge, *huge* poster [of me] in Toronto. I had been taken for a ride." She could take anything, including the bra and underwear job ad through which she had already suffered, but manipulation was something she would not tolerate. The embarrassment of the billboard incident, coupled with her growing disenchantment with the monotony of modeling assignments and constant critical glances, contributed to her quitting the business once and for all.

Not wanting to lose their client altogether, the modeling agency sent Neve out on a round of commercial auditions. For Campbell commercials weren't an extension of modeling, they were a segue into acting. Since *Phantom* Neve had fallen in love with performing. She believed she had a real flair for the dramatic arts, and wanted to test her skills through auditions. She made a pact with herself. If she showed promise as an actress, she would continue in her pursuit of roles. But should she be a washout, Neve vowed to return to her roots as a dancer. She was at a crossroads of sorts, and was happy with following either creative path. To her surprise and her agent's delight, Campbell became the golden child of Canadian casting directors. A natural in front of the camera, the young actress channeled the same depth of emotion that had made her a remarkable dancer into winning many sought-after roles in commercials.

Her first break surfaced in the form of a TV ad for the Eaton Center, a Toronto shopping mall. While her agency was happy to land the plum assignment, Campbell didn't share in their jubilation. "It was a silly little commercial and I only had one line," she explained to *FHM*. "I am with my two little brothers and we are having a hard time trying to decide what to buy our mother for Christmas and I say, 'Hey guys—look what I got mom.' And it's a pair of gloves."

Because all her recent professional coups seemed to come so easy to her, Neve didn't appreciate what all the fuss was about. She couldn't possibly have known that her relative ease in securing commercial jobs was hardly the norm. Yet Neve would once again breeze past the competition and emerge victorious in a tough, competitive career field. Beating out countless other gifted performers would come as no surprise. She had, of course, been doing it most of her life.

In the next five months of 1991, Neve would take the Canadian world of advertising by storm, appearing in one commercial after another. With so many credits to add to her résumé, she was, once again, feeling confident and in control. There was simply no stopping her. The ad campaigns that were graced by her dynamic presence included a Coke commercial with rock icon Bryan Adams. The high cheese factor, however, didn't escape the ambitious dancer-turned-actor's notice. She was well aware of the stigma attached to hocking wares on television. However, like most successful thespians who have gone through the commercial ringer, she accepted it as a temporary and necessary evil.

Born with a wry sense of humor, Neve couldn't resist scoffing at the absurdity of her current line of work, which included a spot for Tampax. "Tampon adverts are the worst, aren't they? They're so unrealistic—like women are going to do all this athletic stuff wearing skin-tight white pants! It's ridiculous, ha ha," she joked with *FHM*. "My commercial was like a gang of silly teenage girls running round school on photo day—you know, when everyone gets their picture taken for the yearbook. They are in this line-up waiting to have their pictures taken and I look in my purse to pull out a hairbrush and my tampons are in there. I look very proud of them."

While pleased with the progress she had made since leaving *Phantom*, Neve was anxious to do work of a higher caliber. She felt she had paid her dues and was ready to take on the challenging world of film and television.

In 1992 Neve's wish to make a greater impact in the acting community came true. With commercials, the nineteen-year-old had been limited to speaking only a few lines oncamera, or not at all. She hoped that the film and television work would provide a better outlet for the acting skills she had been steadily honing. So when Campbell's agent sent her to audition for a new Canadian TV series titled *Catwalk* (1992–93), she was grateful for the chance to prove herself. The producers were immediately impressed by Neve. Not only could she act, but she could sing and dance as well. And since one of the female roles was that of a dance teacher, it seemed that Neve was once again in the right place at the right time. The role of Daisy in the hourlong drama would be hers.

Besides seeking the kind of TV exposure that could propel her career to new heights, Neve legitimately liked the story and concept behind the series. *Catwalk* was set in Toronto, Canada. Revolving around a group of young people in their twenties, the series chronicled the trials and tribulations of a struggling pop band. The story opens with Johnnie Camden (Keram Malicki-Sanchez), a talented guitarist who has become tired of his old group, deciding to recruit new musicians to form a band. Included in this new lineup is Daisy McKenzie (Neve) on keyboards, Mary Owens (Kelli Taylor) on bass guitar, Jesse Carlson (Paul Popowich) on drums, Sierra Williams (Lisa Butler) on vocals, and Atlas Robinson (Christopher Lee Clements) on rap and rhythm. Trying to get their personal and professional lives on track, this band of merry musicians goes about falling in and out of love, finally landing a much-coveted record deal. The production premiered in October 1992 on Canadian network YTV.

As a series regular, Campbell was thrown into a whirlwind of activity. She had never spent so much time in front of the camera, and she took the opportunity to learn everything she could about working on a dramatic series. No matter how hard she labored, however, she couldn't stamp out the artistic differences she was having with the show's producers. She told *TV Guide*, "I played Daisy, a singer and dance teacher. It was a good learning experience because it gave me a lot of onscreen training. But we had problems with the producers and politics. The creator was fired two weeks into the run, so my character was changed from kind of a spiritual chick with a lot to say to this sex symbol instead."

Originally, Campbell loved the characters and the writing, but after the show's creator was dismissed without notice, the game plan was rewritten and nobody bothered to consult the players. Neve felt cheated and hurt by the lack of input she was allowed. The opportunity to play a role so similar to herself had seemed a blessing. That all changed, however, when she was suddenly forced to wear skimpy outfits and prance around the set like a *Playboy* bunny. She described the evolution of her character to *Entertainment Weekly*, "She became the sex symbol. She was sleeping with every character. It was frustrating."

Ever since the Sony ad campaign mishap, playing a sex kitten sat none too well with the dignified young actress. Feeling belittled and taken advantage of, Campbell tried to reach a compromise with her TV producers, but to no avail. Ratings were great, and they were not about to tamper with a winning formula. If anyone seemed to be out of line, it was Neve. From the staff's perspective, she should remain quiet and enjoy the steady income.

Facing such professional opposition couldn't have been easy for the feisty young woman. She had her show business reputation to consider, and if word got out that she had been difficult to work with, it could cost her future acting assignments. Neve vacillated back and forth the whole season, trying to decide whether to stay or quit. That decision became much easier when she began getting perverse fan mail from incarcerated criminals. "I got some weird letters," she cringed during a *Twist* interview, "like a guy who described my mouth and then every part of my body in graphic detail. All I could think [was], 'Umm, when do you get out?' Completely creepy stuff!"

Despite Neve's objections, *Catwalk* went on to develop a loyal Canadian following. YTV ordered a total of twenty-four episodes, but then canceled the series in 1993. "Unfortunately, they're still playing those same twenty-four episodes in Canada. It's got a cult following that I just can't understand," Neve told *FHM*. In March 1994, the show resurfaced when the production team of Franklin Waterman Entertainment bought the rights to create new episodes and broadcast previous episodes in the United States via MTV.

Neve Campbell left after the first season (her character went off to Los Angeles), and the show went through additional cast changes before making its MTV debut. Receiving a favorable response from viewers, *Catwalk* didn't fare so well with the critics. A TV reviewer for *Variety* wrote, "The likeable young cast, for the most part, makes a sincere step at elevating Levy's trite script, but to little avail. The series may find a following among its obviously targeted younger viewers. However, unless its writers focus on issues of greater substance, it will continue to amount to little more than, 'Hey, my uncle's got a barn, let's do a show!'" Failing to live up to the ratings it garnered in Canada, *Catwalk* retired into syndication soon thereafter.

While working on the TV series, Neve had no trouble obtaining roles in film and television. From 1992 to 1993, she made guest appearances on the Canadian-based TV programs *My Secret Identity* (1988–91), *The Kids in the Hall* (1989–94), and the U.S.-produced shows *Are You Afraid of the Dark?* (1992–present) and *Kung Fu: The Legend Continues* (1992–97) with David Carradine. She enjoyed acting in those roles, and, more specifically, the lack of ongoing commitment to a project that guest-starring permitted.

If Neve was going to dedicate herself to something, it would have to be a project with considerable artistic merit. In Canada, however, as elsewhere, it was difficult for a relative newcomer to be considered for the best media productions. Therefore, while Campbell's early TV roles helped pay her bills, they would prove fruitless in satisfying her appetite for quality work. It should not be surprising, therefore, that Neve turned to independent films. At least with those projects she was able to voice her ideas, get feedback, craft a character, and watch it evolve in the course of making the movie. The process of onscreen transformation was what fascinated her the most, and as long as she felt artistically challenged, Neve didn't mind the low pay that often accompanied high standards.

Contrary to popular belief, the horror genre to which Campbell would stay faithful well into her career did not start with *The Craft* (1996), but with another low-budget science-fiction thriller called *The Dark* (1994). In the eighty-seven minute film, the plot thickens when something unspeakable and deadly is discovered beneath the ground in a graveyard. Neve plays Deputy Jesse, who is understandably alarmed when she stumbles upon the giant ratlike creature. She enlists the aid of the only scientist (Scott Wickware) who can save the town from the creature's menacing clutches, and mayhem ensues. Judging from the plot alone, the movie had little chance of becoming a worldwide success. With its low-budget special effects and over-the-top dialogue, the R-rated *The Dark* faded into obscurity shortly after its release.

A reviewer for the Video Graveyard Web site wrote, "Poor effects and a totally lame 'hey let's be sympathetic towards the creature, maybe it's not so bad after all...' finale sinks this dull junk that's only notable for having Neve Campbell (before her turns in the *Scream* movies) in the cast."

Campbell's second foray into the world of independent features was an appearance in *Paint Cans* (1994), a cutting satire on the Canadian film industry. Neve could appreciate the picture's main intent as she, too, had had her fair share of industry-related frustrations, disappointments, and betrayals. The chance to contribute her own voice to the farce was far too tempting to refuse. Created by Canadian filmmaker Paul Donovan, *Paint Cans* follows the path of Vittorio Musso (Bruce Greenwood), a young man who sets out to secure government financing for his independent film, also titled *Paint Cans*. What begins as a criticism of the Canadian Film Board system concludes as a ferocious comedy, complete with a surprise ending.

The film debuted at the Toronto Film Festival and was screened at the American Film Institute Festival in Los Angeles before making its way back to Canada, where it was slated for general release. Critics who praised the performances included a reviewer for the *Arts Atlantic*, who wrote, "The supporting cast is equally strong: Bruce Greenwood (*Exotica*) is convincingly slimy as Vittorio Musso, the filmmaker whose arty project, *Paint Cans*, wreaks havoc on Wick's life; veteran Don Francks is memorable as Wick's cantankerous father; Robyn Stevan strikes a nice balance between guile and innocence as the ambitious young journalist who breaks Wick's heart."

While playing second fiddle was a good way to attach film credits to her name, Neve's chance to headline came in the form of a starring role in the short film *Love Child* (1995), directed, produced, and written by Patrick Sisam. Playing the role of sixteen-year-old Deidre in an era of bell bottoms and lava lamps, Campbell drew upon her own tormented romantic past to give the film's theme of awakened sexuality added resonance. Filling the part of prepubescent Murray's (Dov Tiefenbach) dream girl, Neve could relate to the theme of unrequited love; a sympathy that helped elevate the quality of her onscreen performance. The film went on to earn the Black Maria Film Festival's First Place Juror's Award in

1996, the Hamptons International Film Festival's honor for best screenplay in 1996, and Chicago International Film Festival's Silver Hugo Award in that same year. On March 1, 1999, Atom Films, a newly formed production company, announced plans to release the short film over the Internet.

Campbell's next foray into feature films saw her depicting the life of Nepeese, a half–Native American, half-white girl. The chance to star in a movie with French director Arnaud Sélignac was a high point in her acting career to date. Based on the novel *Baree: Son of Kazan* (1917) by James Oliver Curwood, the film depicts the life of a young woman and her wolf-dog, Baree. The film focuses on the bond between Baree, Nepeese, and her father, Pierre, played by Jacques Weber of *Cyrano de Bergerac* (1990) fame. The story begins with Paul (Jeff Fahey) befriending Nepeese and her father. Suspense mounts when a local trader kills Nepeese's dad in order to secure her hand in marriage. Finally, Paul and Baree team up to save her life. The PG-13–rated film was released later as a U.S. television movie under the title *Northern Passage*.

Ironically, Nepeese wasn't the only one lucky enough to escape with her life. During shooting in 1993, Neve was also caught in a perilous situation. Deciding to have fun with the cast and crew on the set in Montreal, Neve omitted to reveal her proficiency in the French language. Her intention was to listen surreptitiously to people's conversations. On one particular day, with both her mother and brother visiting the set, Campbell was scheduled to shoot a scene with an untamed bear. Assuming the producers and director would not willingly put one of their stars in harm's way, Neve didn't give the scene much thought, that is, until she overheard Arnaud Sélignac discussing the worst case scenarios with the stunt man/bear trainer.

When Campbell discovered how dangerous the scene could become, she panicked. After giving the matter some thought, however, she decided to go along with it, praying that the stunt-man would prevent any possible mishaps. "And we were rehearsing and they told me to put honey on my hand and run," she explained to late night TV talk show host Conan O'Brien. "And I ran, and I turned around. . . . The bear attacked me, and it grabbed me by the leg and dragged me through the forest. And the stunt person had to come and save me, and I was screaming. And my mother and my little brother [Damian] were visiting me on the set that day. It really sucked." Luckily, Neve escaped in the nick of time. Although she would never have admitted as much to the director, the terror she felt during that scene helped her to render a compelling portrayal of her character's abduction.

Working around the clock to build a solid reputation was something Neve had come to terms with. Spending quality time with her live-in lover, Jeff Colt, however, was becoming far more difficult. As an actor, Jeff realized how crucial these years were to Neve's artistic development, and he was both patient and supportive. Neve felt no qualms in taking on more roles than she could handle. If it meant having less time to devote to her relationship, then that was a sacrifice she was quite willing to make. Part of what initially drew the couple together was their mutual need for space and independence. And now that her career was going full-speed ahead, she was not about to change the very quality of her being that Jeff had fallen in love with.

The body of work she had amassed in 1993 enabled her to land pivotal roles in two American made-for-television movies filmed in Canada. Her eye-opening experiences on the sets of NBC's *I Know My Son Is Alive* and CBS's *Janek: The Forget-Me-Not Murders*, which aired in the United States on February 20, 1994, and March 29, 1994, respectively, would be the catalysts in her eventual emigration to the United States. In *Janek*, Neve depicts Jessica Foy, murder victim number eight in a series of grisly homicides. Cast as goddaughter to Frank Janek of the NYPD (played by Richard Crenna) Neve appears in a few brief scenes in the beginning of the TV film. Her role was minor but memorable: Her dialogue consisted solely of a phone message left minutes before her untimely death. *Janek: The Forget-Me-Not Murders* was prophetic on several counts: Campbell would later play an attempted murder victim to a heavy phone-breather in *Scream* (1996), and would be teamed alongside her *Janek* costar Helen Shaver in *The Craft* (1996).

Although Neve eventually ended up calling the Fox network home, it was actually NBC that settled the question of her relocating to the United States. Acting with television veterans and real-life married couple Corbin Bernsen and Amanda Pays in *I Know My Son Is Alive* (1994), Neve filled the part of an impressionable nanny who becomes an accomplice in a husband's attempt to drive his wife insane. When the couple's baby is abducted, all eyes turn to the wife, in whose car a bloodstained baby blanket is discovered.

While displaying her acting mettle in the suspense thriller *I Know My Son Is Alive*—also known as *Web of Deceit*—Neve intrigued the film's producers, who taught her the ins and outs of the entertainment industry. Thus, she got the professional higher learning she was looking for. This time, however, the curriculum would feature Business 101 instead of acting fundamentals. Spotting in the actress a real internal fire and potential for great things, the NBC producers loathed to see Neve laboring helplessly in the relatively narrow arena of opportunities in the Canadian entertainment industry. They had seen many average actresses prosper in the Los Angeles show business community. If less gifted performers could forge successful careers for themselves, surely Neve would have no trouble making her own mark.

Weighing their advice, Neve agreed that the United States would provide her with more professional work. She could not afford to waste a chance to arrive in L.A. under the protection of such powerful industry figures. "Unfortunately, in Canada you can only get so far and then you have to come to the States to be recognized, which is kind of frustrating," Neve reasoned with *In the Mix*. The decision would be one she would struggle with for several weeks. She had to consider Jeff as well as her family ties. Would her relationships withstand the pressures of a long separation?

At the age of twenty, Campbell was forced to make a life-altering choice that would make or break her plans for the future. The pressure was too much to handle, so she alleviated the stress by giving herself a cut-off date. By limiting the time she would spend in Los Angeles, she was able to classify the trip as a vacation rather than a permanent relocation. If her career blossomed, then she would cross that proverbial bridge when she came to it. As Neve realized, even getting a credible agent could prove difficult. "I thought I'd go to Hollywood, get turned down at loads of auditions, and just go home dejected a month later," Neve revealed later in an on-air interview with the Ireland Film and Television network. "That's what every actor is supposed to do. Only the dumb ones stick around." In Los Angeles there were no guarantees. Neve suspected that she would be returning to Canada sooner than either Jeff or her family anticipated.

Five

THE PARTY HAS JUST BEGUN

nlike most would-be starlets coming to Los Angeles for the first time, Neve harbored no naive illusions of overnight success when she arrived on January 24, 1994. Well aware of how perilous the climb from the trenches of obscurity could be, Campbell was not as susceptible to Hollywood's allure as some of her contemporaries. On the other hand, she wasn't a novice to the industry. Her résumé was impressive for a person of her relative youth, and with the recommendation she received from the producers of *I Know My Son Is Alive* (1994), she could probably expect to avoid the typical door-in-the-face welcome experienced by so many show business newcomers.

She quickly learned that in Hollywood nearly everyone is in some way connected to the entertainment industry. "I remember getting off the plane from Toronto in Los Angeles, and talking to the cab driver, and he was like, 'What do you do?' And I was like, 'I'm coming here to act,' and he said, 'Oh yeah, I have a screenplay,'" she commiserated with TV talk show maven Rosie O'Donnell. "And it's just the oddest thing because even the cab drivers are in the business somehow. It gets tedious. It gets really tedious."

Saying goodbye to her live-in boyfriend Jeff Colt in Toronto was probably the most difficult moment of her life. When she arrived in Los Angeles, she was utterly torn. On the one hand, she dreamed of rushing back home to her familiar and loving relationship. On the other, leaving L.A. too soon meant that she couldn't make it in the entertainment business. Whatever the outcome, she knew it would contain some element of pain for her. Whether she would have to cope with the pressures of sudden fame or total oblivion was the only uncertainty.

As if to compound her confusion, the city of Los Angeles was in the throes of its own bout with chaos. Just a week earlier, the city had been shaken by the devastating Northridge earthquake, which measured a sinister 6.7 on the Richter scale. Arriving amidst the rubble, debris, and human tragedy, Neve thought that her plans to secure an agent would have to be put on hold.

Someone less superstitious would have simply chalked up the event to bad timing, but to the actress of Scottish descent the earthquake was a sign of worse to come. It was all she could do to keep from packing her bags and returning home immediately. Something, however, told her to stay put. After all, even a disaster of great magnitude may be taken as a signal to rebuild and create from scratch. Watching local residents pick up the pieces of their lives and start anew inspired Campbell to do the same. Besides, the machine that is Hollywood never breaks down—not even from natural disaster.

Luckily, Neve did not hesitate in searching for an agent. While other talent representatives she contacted chose not to "waste" their time evaluating her past performances and discussing her future objectives with her, Neve did find a sympathetic ear and a helping hand in manager Arlene Forester. When Forester heard about the career deadline Campbell had set for herself, the savvy veteran realized that Neve's wasn't just another case of instant-fame syndrome. The agent wasted no time arranging a flurry of auditions for her new client.

One of the auditions the actress would later be loath to admit attending was for a spot as one of the beachside regulars on the cast of *Baywatch* (1989–present). At the time, Neve was making every attempt to secure work during her limited stay in Los Angeles. It was clear she preferred to work on higher-quality projects, but to keep her manager happy Neve agreed to go under the scrutiny of the show's casting directors. As one of ten thousand *Baywatch* wannabes to audition, Campbell attended a closed casting call led by casting directors Susie Glicksman and Fern Orenstein. Much to her relief, the tough judges thought she wasn't appropriate in either looks or temperament for the TV series, and politely showed her the door. Orenstein later defended her casting decision to *People* magazine. "I didn't think she was right on *Baywatch*. . . . Plus she is pale. That wouldn't work." The last thing Neve was aspiring to become was the quintessential *Baywatch* babe so she gladly took her leave.

Unwilling to let the failure of her first Hollywood audition lower her spirits, the young actress remained eager to find a project she could relate to. It was during her first week in town that her manager, Arlene, recommended that Neve audition for a new dramatic series for the Fox network. While feature films would have been Campbell's top acting choice, working on a television show would help her secure her necessary immigration green card. Realizing she was in no position to be overly selective, Neve sat down to read the TV script in its entirety.

Much to her surprise, the writing exceeded all her expectations. And when Forester informed her that the show would be produced by the writer of one of Neve's favorite TV series, she agreed to try out without a moment of hesitation. "I used to watch *The Wonder Years* [1988–93] all the time. I loved that show," she told *TV Guide*. "I just think it was an incredibly written show and the quality is really wonderful. And when I originally read the

script for *Party of Five*, my manager told me it was the same producer as the one who wrote *Wonder Years*, Ken Topolsky, and
that's what made me so enthusiastic about the show."

The commercial merit of the TV project was secondary to
Neve. Her main objective was to contribute to a show that would
make an impact on viewers' lives. On *Catwalk*, back in Toronto,
she had seen firsthand her fair share of smoke, mirrors, fantasy,
and glamour. The cinema verité feel of *Party of Five* was a welcome
break from the high-gloss factor of that series. "The writers have
always been less interested in the glamour and look of the show
than in the emotions and growth of the characters," she described
Party of Five to *Cosmopolitan* magazine.

While evaluating the pilot, Neve discerned the meticulous
attention paid to character development. That fact made the idea
of playing a girl five years her junior far more palatable. The
oncamera role of Julia Salinger, a vulnerable fifteen-year-old
orphan, struck a deep chord in Neve. Julia's fictional history
closely resembled her own path toward maturity, and she drew
on her past experiences to prepare for the audition. "Julia's very
much like me. I'm a very stubborn person," she relayed to *Tiger
Beat* in 1995. "I'm quite open to people's emotions and stuff but
when it comes to doing what I want to do, I do it. Julia's very
much that way, too."

High on Campbell's list of favorite things about *Party* was its
subject matter. The plot concerned five orphans, ranging in age
from one to twenty-four, trying to make sense of their lives in the
absence of parents, who had died in a car crash. "That's the great
thing about *Party of Five*," she informed *Soap Opera Digest*. "The
characters aren't perfectly happy; they make mistakes. It's a realistic situation; they don't have parents to look up to."

Having moved out of her family home to reside with her
brother Christian at an early age, Campbell had some insight

into the TV family's state of mind. After all, she had been making her own decisions for quite some time. She had also made her own share of mistakes along the way. Reading the *Party of Five* script, Neve realized that this was the first time she had so closely identified with a television show. After spending several sleepless nights preparing for the big audition, she knew that what had begun as little more than a means of staying in the United States had become a matter of far greater importance.

Casting the series roles of Claudia, Charlie, and Bailey Salinger already had taken its toll on *Party of Five* co-creators Amy Lippman and Christopher Keyser. Finding the perfect actress to fill Julia's angst-ridden shoes, however, proved to be the ultimate challenge for the duo. They, along with the show's producers and casting directors, had sorted through over three hundred résumés and headshots—yet something—or rather, someone was missing.

Many of the actresses who read for the pilot were genuinely talented. That, however, was not enough to sway the casting vote. In order to win the key part of Julia, the actress would not only have to be a solid performer in her own right, but she would also have to conform to the Salingers' group dynamic. "We had a terrible time casting Julia. The [Fox] network was extremely concerned that every family member really fit," Chris Keyser, co-creator and executive producer, elaborated to *TV Guide*. "If any one of them wasn't right, it would undermine everything we were working for in dramatizing the struggles of this family to survive together. And we had auditioned hundreds of actresses for Julia without finding one that Fox liked." Amy Lippman seconded that notion, telling *People Online*, "Chris and I were both involved in casting the show. It took a long time and was very hard. It was hard to find people who looked like they were family, which was one of the most important criteria for hiring the cast."

Arriving at the audition not a moment too soon, Campbell was stunned by the anxiety apparent on everyone's faces. The audition process was coming to a close, and the pressure was visibly mounting. "Neve walked in the door on a Monday afternoon. We only had two days to find our Julia and have her read with all of the family regulars for Fox before we flew to Vancouver to film the pilot," Keyser continued.

The young actress knew very little of what was going on behind the scenes of the *Party of Five* project, but she could feel the tension in the air as she read before a crowd of onlookers. "It was a little overwhelming at first because I didn't know there would be about forty people packed in the room and everyone is staring at you," she reported to *TV Guide*, "but I actually enjoy auditioning because I like performing."

Neve had unknowingly sealed her destiny on *Party of Five*. Everyone from the Fox executives to the show's writers and producers were taken aback by her reading. Peter Roth, the president of the Fox network, would later rave to the *Los Angeles Times*, "Neve is magic, pure magic. She's beautiful, she's accessible, she's a sensational actress. She has a quality people can relate to, that they can embrace and feel for."

After Neve left the audition room, it would only take another five minutes for the assembled parties to reach a unanimous decision. Few words were even exchanged. It was as if a heavenly spirit had breezed in and solved all their casting woes. Campbell was the performer they had been searching for. "Neve read for two minutes, and that was it. She was Julia," Keyser told *TV Guide*. "We couldn't believe that it happened so suddenly after all that time, so we called the casting director to book Neve immediately."

Neve, meanwhile, was convinced she had blown her chance of appearing in the forthcoming TV series. The audition seemed all too brief, and being cut off midstream could only mean one thing in her estimation: rejection. When the producers informed Neve of their decision to bring her on as a cast regular, she needed a few moments to recover her senses. Not only had she not struck out, she had won the coveted part.

It was quite natural that Neve should be unprepared for her good fortune. She had only been in Los Angeles for two weeks. The most she had hoped to achieve in that time frame was to hire an agent and do a few auditions. Landing a role in a network TV series was not something she had even allowed herself to imagine. Describing the happy event to *Sassy*, Campbell was reluctant to base her success on mere luck or chance. "I've worked very hard to get where I am, so I don't believe it was handed to me on a silver platter," she said.

Neve had no time to weigh the pros and cons of joining the Fox family. The producers needed her decision immediately, as they were anxious to start taping the pilot in Vancouver, British Columbia, Canada (a temporary shooting location selected to save on production costs). On one hand, Neve was grateful for the opportunity to act in a TV series. On the other, she worried about committing herself to any one project for a long period of time. Making up her mind in a matter of minutes, her decision was a definitive "Yes!"

She reasoned that since the majority of pilots are never picked up for actual season runs of TV, her time on *Party of Five* would be limited. Meanwhile she could extend her stay in Los Angeles and see what other career offers turned up. She never guessed that in six years she would still be toiling away on the set of *Party of Five*. "The reason why I took *Party of Five* was not just because it was well-written, but also so I could get into the country from Canada and get my face seen," Neve told *Twist*. "I didn't expect it to continue, let alone go this far."

The creation of *Party of Five* is as interesting a tale as the one it depicts on television. Devised by veteran scribes Amy Lippman and Chris Keyser, the series took a long and winding path to become what it is today—a much-beloved show that die-hard TV fans gladly work their schedules around to watch.

When Amy Lippman and Chris Keyser met at Harvard University, they were just two young adults with a dream to write superb television shows. A disillusioned third-year law school student, Chris decided to concentrate on writing. He met Amy, who was then an undergraduate, in a playwriting course. The two became friends and made their way separately to New York City in 1985, where Amy's writing expertise helped her land a position on *Loving* (1983–95), a daytime soap opera. Chris, on the other hand, wasn't getting the writing jobs he wanted.

In 1988 Lippman and Keyser made the decision to team up professionally and move to Los Angeles to pursue their entertainment careers full force. The dynamic duo hammered out a spec script for *The Wonder Years* (1988–93). Although the offering was rejected by the *Wonder Years'* producers, it was routed to Steven Bochco, the co-creator of *L.A. Law* (1986–94) and *Hill Street Blues* (1981–87). He, in turn, gave it to David E. Kelley, who was then producing *L.A. Law*. Their top-notch writing earned the ambitious pair a spot on *L.A. Law's* writing staff. That, according to Lippman, "was a great show to write for, it made it safer for other producers to hire us to write for their shows."

With such an impressive TV series writing credit, Amy and Chris became the most vied-after writing team since Harry and Linda Bloodworth Thomason of *Designing Women* (1986–93) sitcom fame. A writing stint on the long-lived dramatic series *Sisters* (1991–96) was quick in the coming. Working on that hourlong show, Amy and Chris diligently studied the production process. They ached to branch out on their own, but were well aware of the difficulties of selling a television network on a new series. In November 1994, they brainstormed some show concepts and had several meetings with Fox network executives. To the team's chagrin, the network just wasn't biting. That's why when Fox approached the two with its own concept, Amy and Chris jumped at the golden opportunity.

While it was late in the development season for the new TV year (1994–95), Fox had definite ideas about the kind of fare they wanted to air. They were anxious to see a treatment for a show that would feature a family of orphans free of parental constraints. Lippman recalled the experience, "Initially Fox came to us with the idea of doing a show about kids living on their own. That's the only thing they gave us to go on."

To say that they had their work cut out for them would be a gross understatement. The only thing they were certain of was that Fox wanted the show to be similar to its steamy counterparts *Beverly Hills, 90210* (1990–present) and *Melrose Place* (1992–99). Since creating a TV show about fun-loving orphans was inconceivable to the integrity-driven writers, they devised instead an entry with grit and substance. "Both of our spouses lost parents very early in life and I think both Chris and I have drawn off their experience," Lippman pointed out during a Viewers Voice organization interview. "Certainly there are story lines that I have taken directly from my husband's life and dramatized because they are very real and very moving."

Fox had provided the basic concept, but Lippman and Keyser would contribute their own signature style to the potential show. They were determined to steer clear of fluffy material and to break down social boundaries in the process. "We thought about it for a couple weeks, and we gave them a show that was probably a little darker and more real than what they had envisioned when they came to us," Lippman reflected during a *People* interview.

When the two writers finally pitched the show, Fox wasn't at all prepared for what it heard. The network had anticipated something far more upbeat than a somber drama about reality-based orphans (who albeit do own prime San Francisco real estate, as well as their own restaurant). That's when Lippman and Keyser made the historical argument that changed the face of teen-oriented American television forever. They felt that if the writing and character development continued to be of the highest possible quality, home viewers would respond. It was as simple as that. In the end, the co-creators compromised with the network. "We were thinking it should be more fun and light, while Chris and Amy really wanted to mine the dramatic side of it," Fox executive vice presidnet Bob Greenblatt told *Entertainment Weekly*. "But they were willing to do both, so we said, 'Go ahead.'"

A celebratory mood was in the air. *Party of Five* would have a chance to compete for a prime-time slot. But Chris and Amy soon learned that a long and arduous process lay ahead of them. They would need to cast the show, produce a winning pilot, and then weather the nail-biting period before the network announced its new fall lineup.

First on their list of priorities was the casting process, which ended up taking far longer than anyone had anticipated. After searching far and wide for just the right players, it was announced that Scott Wolf (as Bailey, age sixteen), Lacey Chabert (as Claudia, age eleven), Matthew Fox (as Charlie, age twenty-four), Neve Campbell (as Julia, age fifteen), and Zachary and Alexander Ahnert (alternating as Owen, age one) would be the new Salinger family. (After the pilot episode was filmed, Brandon and Taylor Porter took over the role of Owen from the Ahnert twins. After the first season, they, in turn, were replaced by Andrew and Steven Cavarno for subsequent seasons and, later on in the series, by Jacob Smith.)

It was in February 1994, while shooting the pilot in Vancouver, that the now well-known camaraderie enjoyed by the cast first became apparent. While bonding and establishing chemistry is important to any ensemble-driven show, it was critical to the success of *Party of Five*. The whole program centered around the Salingers, so, in order to deliver a convincing performance, the players had to instantly connect and act like a family. "We all went off to Vancouver together and lived there together for about six weeks, away from everyone else, sort of locked in the hotel together," Keyser said during a speech at the Museum of Television & Radio in October 1996. "And got to know each other 'like a family.' Starting that way, all together, away from all the other distractions, I think it created some kind of atmosphere, particularly among the cast."

Once the pilot was completed, it was back to Los Angeles to await Fox's verdict on whether or not they would pick *Party of Five* for the upcoming 1994–95 season. In May 1994, Fox selected the programs to air. *Party of Five* was one of six series to be given the green-light. Surviving its first year, however, was by no means an easy proposition for the series' makers.

The pilot was routed to reviewers before it was unveiled to the general public on Monday, September 12, 1994. *USA Today's* Matt Roush hailed the show, writing, "If you are at all inclined to fall for a new TV family of considerable charm and four-handkerchief heart, by all means crash *Party of Five*." Other critics compared the orphan-centered drama with another newcomer, ABC-TV's *My So-Called Life* (starring Claire Danes, A. J. Langer, and Jared Leto), proclaiming both as the best new shows to grace the small screen. But even though *Party of Five* earned the most critical acclaim of any new Fox show, it was still considered the most dubious of the fall lineup. "We didn't feel it *wasn't* right for Fox," Fox executive Bob Greenblatt reported to *Entertainment*

Weekly. "We were nervous that it wasn't quite as high-concept, quite as sexy, quite as cool as *90210*."

Greenblatt's concerns had validity, especially considering the fact that *Party of Five* was a Nielsen ratings disaster, landing in the lowest ranks of prime-time shows. (Because Fox, a relatively new TV network, had fewer station affiliations, their programming was available to far fewer potential home viewers than other networks, and, thus, automatically could not compete successfully in the ratings with ABC, CBS, and NBC.)

During its first year, the cast, production crew, and creators sat on pins and needles, praying that the weekly show be allowed to continue. The threat of cancellation was very real, as described by Lippman to *People*, "Obviously, for years we thought it could be canceled at any minute. We've had to come to terms with having a kind of moderate hit on our hands."

The first season of *Party of Five* depicts the struggles of five orphans trying to pick up the pieces of their lives after their parents are killed in a tragic car accident. During the debut season, Bailey becomes dangerously attracted to a waitress addicted to drugs, Charlie comes to terms with his new parental role, Julia overcomes her academic slump, and the Salingers confront the drunk driver responsible for their parents' deaths. In short, the first twenty-two episodes poignantly established the family's moral and emotional foundation.

During the 1994 TV year, the cast was having difficulties concentrating on the task at hand. Giving his take on the proverbial axe hanging over their heads, Scott Wolf told Entertainment Weekly, "It was so frustrating. You start to think, 'Am I pouring my heart into something that will be gone next week?'" The atmosphere was not exactly conducive to creative endeavor, but the cast continued to plug away, hoping for the best but expecting the worst.

A light at the end of the tunnel came in the form of John Matoian, who took on his responsibilities as Fox Entertainment president several weeks into the show's first season. Expressing his commitment to quality programming, Matoian allayed some of the group's fears. Investing more money into *Party of Five*'s promotional budget, Matoian gave *Party of Five* a new lease on television. The series was slotted Monday nights at 9:00 P.M. following *Melrose Place*, opposite ABC's *Monday Night Football*, CBS's sitcoms *Murphy Brown* and *Love & War*, and NBC's *Monday Movie*. "I think that we have a fantastic time slot, coming after *Melrose* and opposite football, which is obviously one of the strongest programs of the week," Keyser said to Viewers Voice. "On the other hand, it probably doesn't necessarily appeal to quite the same type of audience that our show does."

The show, however, didn't fare quite as well as was anticipated, and was reshuffled to a new time slot of 9:00 P.M. on Wednesday nights following *Beverly Hills, 90210*. (Its new competition in this time period included ABC's sitcoms *Roseanne* and *Ellen*, CBS's *Touched by an Angel*, and NBC's *Dateline*.) Earning only one ratings point over its average of 6.1 that night, *Party of Five* was gaining quickly a place on everyone's endangered-series list. Alarming the fans as to the show's precarious state, *USA Weekend* ran a long article in January 1995, inciting the troops to support their favorite band of orphans. Over fifteen thousand letters of support poured in to the magazine's office. Viewers had fallen in love with the Salinger family, and they were not about to sit by and idly watch their party break up.

The first special Wednesday night episode on November 2, 1994, may not have set off any sparks in the ratings department, but it did bring a new group of viewers on board. Slowly, the ratings began to rise, showing a significant increase in the important demographic of adults aged eighteen to thirty-four. But, by the end of the first season *Party of Five* was still in trouble, ranking 123rd of all network shows. Despite the poor standing, Fox executive John Matoian noticed signs of life and announced the network's commitment to renewing the struggling property. "We have key demographics, very strong for ages 18–34 and overall 18–49. We get very strong responses from college students, who watch in groups, and of course the Nielsens don't cover them," Matoian told *TV Guide*. "We also get a lot of good feedback from teenagers, especially girls. In terms of other Fox dramas, the history is that they build slowly. We're not doing any worse than *90210* or *Melrose Place* in their first seasons."

While the show continued into a second season (1995–96) with an improved ratings average of 7.1, *Party of Five* still had its share of struggles to overcome. Gradually, the numbers started heating up, and by the third season (1996–97), the much-talked about episode, "Hitting Bottom" (February 26, 1997), brought in an impressive 9.6 rating. (In the episode, the story arc of Bailey's alcoholism reaches its peak when Bailey drives drunk and his girlfriend, Sarah Reeves [Jennifer Love Hewitt], is injured when their jeep crashes. An emotionally distraught Bailey visits Sarah in the hospital and begs for help.) That coup, coupled with a Golden Globe Award for best television drama, as well as raves in *Time*, *USA Today*, and *TV Guide*, helped the series finally find its legs. "The show was on a roll," Greenblatt told *Entertainment Weekly*. "It was getting more romantic, more adult, a little sexier. There was still a fight internally about the ratings not being high enough, but everybody said: 'We've got to have it on the air. It's expanding how people think of [Fox].'" With that, *Party of Five* cast aside its most-endangered status, and gave everyone who'd worked so hard on the show a reason to continue to party.

Six

IN FULL SWING

hey say tragedy brings people together. The critical condition of *Party of Five* during its first two seasons allowed its cast to forge solid bonds and unite in an important cause. Initially, Neve had been skeptical about getting close to her coworkers, having had some unpleasant experiences while working on *Catwalk* back in Canada in 1992. Her intimacy issues, however, were quickly dispelled when she encountered the warmth and genuine consideration shown by every member of the cast.

Having left Canada at a moment's notice to move to Los Angeles, Neve was a stranger in a strange land. With no support network to speak of, she was grateful for the companionship and empathy offered by her fun-loving associates. "I feel very fortunate—because we work together intensely and it is important that we get along," she told her fan club. "In many ways we have become a sort of 'pseudo-family' off the set as well. Most of us are in L.A. alone, away from our families, so it is good to have support and cooperation."

Realizing that she wasn't alone in her isolation, Campbell began reaching out to her new family. Twelve-year-old Lacey Chabert, who played thirteen-year-old Claudia on the series, was also having a rough time adjusting to her new environment. Often it was Lacey who managed to bring Neve out of her shell, and the two girls were soon inseparable on the set. "Lacey looks up to Neve like an older sister. From show one, they were singing and dancing off camera, and Neve was carrying Lacey around on her back, having a ball," co-creator Christopher Keyser described the cast to *TV Guide*. "This isn't any cynical bunch of people who've been in the business forever and want nothing to do with each other away from work. They're all fairly new to L.A., they're all at turning points in their careers, and I think they really love each other as friends."

Besides the friendship she formed with Lacey, Campbell was also close to the rest of the cast, all of whom had been similarly struggling to make names for themselves. Matthew Fox (Charlie) was a twenty-seven-year-old actor who had played an athlete in the TV series *Freshman Dorm* (1992) and the 1993 feature film *My Boyfriend's Back*. Twenty-five-year-old Scott Wolf (Bailey) had made some memorable appearances in Burt Reynolds's TV series *Evening Shade* in 1993, and starred in the silly futuristic feature film *Double Dragon* (1994). Lacey Chabert (Claudia) had worked professionally since the age of nine, appearing as Cosette in the Broadway production of *Les Miserables* from 1991 to 1993, and as Bianca Montgomery in 1993 in the long-running ABC soap opera *All My Children* (1970–present). Jennifer Love Hewitt, who joined the *Party of Five* cast when she was fifteen years old in 1995, also had her share of past professional triumphs, with a role in *Sister Act 2: Back in the Habit* (1993), *House Arrest* (1996), and a regular spot on Disney's *Kids Incorporated*, from 1989 to 1991.

While all of the show's stars had amassed impressive acting credits, competition and professional jealousy were never an issue on the set. The cast's mutual belief in the series allowed them to work as a team.

The *Party of Five* cast would often gather for Saturday night dinners at each other's homes in order to unwind after a long week of shooting at the Sony Pictures lot in Los Angeles. A healthy portion of good-natured ribbing and horsing around managed to keep everyone grounded. "We played a lot of basketball and had a lot of long, around-the-table conversations," Scott Grimes, who plays Bailey's best friend Will McCorkle, told *People*. "We became such good friends, and it kind of showed when we filmed the show."

Talking about business off the set was, and continues to be, strictly off-limits. The only rule enforced by the production crew was for everyone to have a good time and enjoy the process, as evidenced by an incident in which Neve was given her new nickname. "There was a scene in the first season where I went 'Hugggh' out of nowhere for no reason whatsoever," she confessed to *US*. "They said, 'Cut!' and everybody just looked at me and said, 'What was that?' So now I'm Foghorn. I laugh like that every once in a while when I'm uncomfortable."

The advantages of working on *Party of Five* outweighed the difficulty of working fifteen-hour days. For Campbell, getting the chance to deliver well-written dialogue was one of the many elements that made her appreciate her role on the series. "Not only is it a great cast, but it's really wonderful to work on a show where every week you get a script you're ecstatic about," she told *Tiger Beat*. "That's really unusual. It's a great experience for any actor to be able to create from something that's already fantastic. It makes your job a lot easier."

The fact that her character was dealing with real issues that concerned real people motivated her to work even harder. "It's a lot of responsibility," Neve expressed to *Sassy*. "Julia goes through circumstances that a lot of girls go through. There's a lot of stuff happening in her life. She takes responsibility for her actions, even if she has been having more than her fair share of stuff to deal with. When you're a teenager, there's a tragedy every day."

While filming *Catwalk* back in Canada, Neve had found herself in the difficult position of having to fight to preserve the integrity of her character. Fortunately, because *Party of Five*'s producers and writers feel an immense responsibility to the series, she has been able to take off her boxing gloves and concentrate on delivering her lines. The show's writers have even gone so far as to collaborate with her when planning pivotal moments in Julia's life. "When it comes to important issues, they do talk with me. Like when Julia lost her virginity. I was somewhat skeptical about it because she got drunk and just did it," she told *Sassy*. "But obviously, she ends up having to deal with the consequences of her actions. Her pregnancy was a big risk for the producers, but it was necessary, considering how irresponsible she was."

With such a cooperative working atmosphere surrounding her every day, Neve found herself in the enviable position of contributing to the show in a way she had never expected. Not only was the production staff open to her comments, they even went out of their way to gather input from Neve and her costars. A rarity in television today, *Party of Five* is special in that it truly practices the family values it preaches.

Party of Five may have struggled to find an audience during its first seasons on the air, but the cast had no trouble establishing their dominance in a teen-driven market. Before *Party of Five* earned a coveted spot on the December 1995 cover of *Time* magazine, the cast, including Neve, had somehow managed to find their way into the spotlight. Making their promotional rounds through malls and state fairs across America, the players were often bombarded by hordes of screaming fans clamoring for their attention. From a virtual unknown to an "overnight" sensation, Neve was caught in a whirlwind of promotional activity that had become both a blessing and a curse.

Neve's oncamera depiction of Julia Salinger earned her a dedicated following among younger TV viewers. With thousands of letters pouring in weekly, the young actress became every teenage girl's inspiration and consternation. Whether Julia had gotten herself into yet another scrape on the air or managed to rise above her plot line circumstances, fans could relate to the often misguided and sometimes vulnerable character. From stealing her best friend's boyfriend to losing her virginity while intoxicated, Julia was an imperfect television heroine, which made her all the more captivating. "People respond to Julia mainly because she's very confused about life and doesn't have it all together," Neve told *Cosmopolitan*. "They relate to that. She's insecure about herself, friendships, and relationships. And who isn't?"

Campbell's girl-next-door appeal also helped cinch her popularity with young female viewers. Tired of the dressed-up glamour kittens parading onscreen, the female constituency welcomed Neve's minimalist approach to hair and makeup with open arms. With a reception this warm, she found it difficult to believe that the show was initially a ratings disaster. "I don't understand why the ratings aren't higher. Everyone I talk to, even on the streets, says, 'This is my favorite show.' I got tons of mail from girls who are Julia's age or younger and relate to her vulnerability and her confusion," she explained to *TV Guide*. "I even got older couples in their sixties who worry about me, they say, 'Are you alright? Can we adopt you?' Well, they're a little confused, but at least they're watching."

Prior to participating in the *Party of Five* mall tour organized by Fox's head honcho, John Matoian, in October 1994, Neve had little exposure to her adoring public. Save for a few avid fans who would wait outside the Sony studio for an autograph, she was a complete stranger to the celebrity promotional circuit. Upon first hearing about the tour, Neve had mixed feelings. She knew how important the appearances could be to the show's success, but feared the public scrutiny. While the actress had already gotten used to being recognized on the streets of Canada for her role in *Catwalk*, fame in the U.S. seemed to exact a bigger price. Putting her reservations on hold, Neve committed herself to supporting the show any way she could.

The tour was one of the most educational experiences of her life. She would never again wonder what it would feel like to be admired, adored, and worshipped by millions. At her first mall visit, Neve expected to see a few hundred people in attendance. To her utter amazement, thousands of girls had camped out, waiting to scream the eardrums off the *Party of Five* stars. Taking in the crowds and posters and homemade signs fluttering in the air, Neve was confronted with one of the most exhilarating and terrifying moments of her life.

"It was trippy having thousands of teenage girls screaming and crying and grabbing," she revealed to *TV Guide*. "I mean, all of a sudden you feel like a rock star and then you realize that you're not, that you're in people's living rooms once a week, and they sit on their couches and they watch you so they feel that they know you. It's understandable that they get excited, but it's overwhelming. It's an odd experience because I think all of us, as actors, think about what it is to be famous and what it is to be a celebrity and what will that experience be, and there is really no describing it when it happens."

The thrill of those first crazy career moments during the 1994–95 season would wear off sooner than Neve had anticipated. Partly responsible for her gradual disenchantment was the difficult schedule she was forced to adhere to. After spending all week filming, Neve had to forsake the quiet weekends she had once cherished in order to make promotional appearances on the show's behalf.

Traversing many cities in a month's time, Neve literally didn't know if she was coming, going, or already there. "I've been to many states in this country, and I can't even tell you which ones they are," she recalled to the *Los Angeles Times*. "When I travel, people ask, 'Have you been here before?' and I say, 'I think I may have. I recognize the airport, I've seen that mall before.' But you don't see anything else! You fly out that day and fly back that night, and all you see are thousands of people who want your autograph."

A hectic lifestyle was one of the first compromises Neve would make for fame. Her privacy, as she soon found out, would also have to be sacrificed on the altar of the Hollywood gods. While her early *Party of Five* glory hadn't even come close to the eminence she would later receive via the *Scream* trilogy, Neve was already feeling the pressures of living under a perpetual spotlight. "It's okay when people come up on the street and say, 'I love your show,' but in a public bathroom? That is something else," she explained to *Cosmopolitan*. "Fans have knocked on the stall to get an autograph. Some people have no tact at all."

Being a role model has its privileges, but Neve could never see past its limitations. As Julia Salinger, Neve was expected to represent teenage girls everywhere, but she was adamantly opposed to sacrificing her growth as an artist for the good of the moral majority. "People always ask, 'What's it like to be looked up to by teens?' It's a wonderful position to be in. It's wonderful that people look up to me and that they can learn things from Julia," Neve professed to *US*. "But on the other hand, I'm an artist. It's like, where's the line? I'm a human being and I'm Neve before I'm anything else. And I'm not going to pretend to be anything I don't want to. This business takes up so much of your life as it is that you shouldn't give up yourself."

Her polar opposite and role model-in-waiting, younger Jennifer Love Hewitt (Sarah Reeves, Bailey's girlfriend) was of a different mind-set, telling *Movieline* magazine, "I like knowing that people look up to me. I know from being a teenager how hard it is to find some-one you can look up to, put your faith, love and excitement into. I like being a normal, approachable person and I like playing them, too."

It wasn't so much that Campbell didn't want to be the voice of her generation, it was more that she was reticent to pay the price with her privacy. As things stood she was already lacking the seclusion she would need to dine in a restaurant undisturbed, to buy groceries without being followed, or to even go to the bath-room alone. Introspective by nature, she found herself in the uncomfortable position of having to dodge the bullets of fan adu-lation everywhere she went.

The perils of fame was a subject that Neve would soon come to know all to well. In the meantime, she trudged along, hoping to maintain the same level of commitment to her craft. In Tinsel-town, where one night can be all that stands between obscurity and worldwide recognition, nothing is ever what it seems. Worried that she might be carried away by the attention, hype, and prom-ises that threatened to engulf her, Neve secretly vowed to keep her feet firmly planted in the soil of reality. "In this business you can get caught up in all the things swirling around you, all the people telling you how special you are," she revealed to *Mademoiselle*. "If you listen to them and believe everything they say, the real you would cease to exist. So I always thought I should base how good I am on how good I feel I am."

As unaffected as Neve was by all the hype, promotion, and hoopla of those early *Party* years from 1994 to 1996, she could not be non-chalant when it came to the series' critical acclaim. Being part of a quality show that critics and fans alike were openly rooting for was a dream come true, especially when that dream placed her on the cover of *Time* magazine. Branded as "one of the six reasons to watch television" by a reviewer, the show and the collective egos behind it were given a tremendous boost by the favorable write-up. "That was really sweet," Neve recalled during a *Genre* interview. "I didn't know it happened and people started calling and congratulating me. And all I could think of was, 'My picture's next to Grandpa Simpson.' I mean, Grandpa Simpson's awesome, but you can't take it too seriously."

While she had always tried to stay calm and unaffected, Neve gladly gave up the fight for composure upon attending the fifty-third annual Golden Globe Award's ceremony on January 21, 1996. The thrill of *Party of Five* beating out heavyweight competition (*ER*, *Chicago Hope*, *NYPD Blue*, and *Murder One*) in the Best Television Drama Series category was something she never thought she would experience so early in her career. Neve couldn't help but be impressed with helping the series to earn the unexpected award.

For one brief night, she let down her guard and allowed herself to enjoy the perks of being a celebrity. Hobnobbing with some of her biggest idols during the course of the evening was a special treat. She told *Sassy*, "I met so many people that night. It was a trip because as I was walking up to the stage, someone tapped me on the shoulder and said, 'Congratulations.' I was like, 'Thanks,' and when I turned around, it was Tom Hanks! Later on, Brad Pitt told Lacey [Chabert] that he loves our show and was so happy we won. It was amazing to realize that these people watch the show and know who we are! That night was extremely surreal."

The acclaim was like a much-needed balm for her childhood wounds. Yet she didn't have to wait until the night of the Golden Globes to receive the positive feedback she was working so hard to attain. Ever since her first day on the set, Neve had become a much-loved and admired figure among her coworkers. Unaware of the tremendous impact her generosity, talents, and struggles made on the *Party of Five* production team, Neve was just glad that people weren't calling her names behind her back as they had in bygone years. The truth is people *were* constantly talking about her. They simply couldn't help it. With so many positive things to say, it was a wonder they had time to talk of anything or anyone else.

One of her biggest champions is Peter Roth, the president of the Fox network. "I'm looking at her picture as we speak, there's a poster for the show on my wall," he told the *Los Angeles Times*. "Neve is magic, pure magic. She's beautiful, she's accessible, she's a sensational actress. She has a quality people can relate to, that they can embrace and feel for. I was watching *Party of Five* the other night, and there was a scene in which I out-and-out wept, simply because of Neve." Executive producer Amy Lippman also testified to the actress's dramatic prowess and expert portrayal of Julia Salinger. "She's technically extraordinarily proficient," she told the *Los Angeles Times*. "If you look at our scripts, she gets a lot of lines like, 'I, dot-dot-dot'—or just, 'But [pause], what?' And she nails every ellipsis. It seems as though she's been doing this for thirty years."

While Neve's onscreen presence touched everyone who saw the show, exposing her offscreen sorrows to her coworkers was difficult for her. The closeness she shared with her new friends on the set eventually made her feel more comfortable about revealing her innermost sentiments, desires, and apprehensions. This newfound openness not only helped her grow as an actress, but also as a person. "Neve's amazing," Jeremy London (who plays Griffin Holbrook) told *Rolling Stone*. "She came from a rough life and has managed to turn lemons into lemonade."

Armed with new friends, a new life, and critical acclaim, Neve was just beginning to find herself as an actress and a celebrity. Although professionally she had never been so satisfied, she almost craved the insecurity and struggle of her early years that had always kept her on her professional toes. Everything had come so easy to her in L.A., including a great new job and loving friends. It seemed almost too good to be true.

One of the biggest obstacles standing in the way of her assimilation into L.A.'s lifestyle was its flawlessness. As an artist, Neve realized the dangers of feeling complacent and nurtured. She worried about sliding into a comfort zone, wherein growth was impossible and experimentation unnecessary. Why would she want to try something new when it could mean a change for the worse? Neve's disorientation, in a town where plastic smiles, plastic bodies, and fake friendships were a matter of course, was apparent from the outset. "When I first came to L.A., I had to change my very cynical and sarcastic humor," she confided in the *Toronto Sun*. "I put a few girls in tears, because they didn't understand."

The shift to a more bubblegum mentality may have given Neve something to complain about during her first year in Los Angeles, but it was the pain of missing her family and boyfriend, Jeff Colt, that finally got the better of her. No matter what she did or how much she accomplished, not having someone to love nearby diminished the impact of those triumphant moments. Staying in touch by phone and receiving the occasional visitor just wasn't enough; nor was the presence of her new friends from *Party of Five* sufficient to raise her spirits consistently. When she was asked in an interview with *Genre* whether she would like to be a superhero, Neve's response indicated the separation anxiety she was experiencing as a result of her fame. "Superheroes are very powerful, but it could make for a lonely life. Just like this business. So, if you can have someone with you, doing it with you, that's perfect."

At length, Neve's wish came true. Christian Campbell's confidence was buoyed by his sister's success, and he arrived to try his own luck in La-La Land. A former acting student from Toronto,

Neve's brother was now anxious to launch a professional career. Having someone familiar from her past at hand made Neve feel much more secure. She and Christian would hang out, talk about auditions, and even test for the same projects. The new relationships Neve had made couldn't compare with the comfort she felt being around Christian. Suddenly, Los Angeles didn't seem to be the farthest place from home. "I'm not very fond of Los Angeles, but I've also been working so much that I haven't really had time to give it a chance," Neve admitted to *Canadian TV Guide* in August 1996. "I've met a few people this year who are wonderful and I'm starting to feel more comfortable. It's great having [Christian] here, we're both going for auditions in which our characters are supposedly love interests! That's the only time when it's been kind of weird."

The only thing that was missing for Neve was having Jeff Colt by her side. While in Canada, the actor had to keep himself busy to cope with the trying separation from his ladylove. He secured a job as host on a popular YTV network show, *It's Alive!* After completing that stint, he was at odds as to what his next move should be. He desperately wanted to move to Los Angeles to be with Neve and to pursue acting, but, unfortunately, he couldn't get a green card to work in the U.S. Even Neve, who was now paying hefty taxes to the American government, had to spend years trying to secure her legal resident status while relying on a work permit to keep her legally in the States. "It only took me four years to get it," she explained to the *Buffalo News*. "It cost me $50,000 [in attorney's fees], and the really crazy thing is that they were denying me the green card even while I was paying $500,000 a year in taxes. It wasn't fair."

With her brother in town and her Shi Tzu dog, Buster, to keep her company, Neve was beginning to believe that she could start a new life in Los Angeles. Just as she was adapting to her new environs, however, she signed on to star in the ABC network made-for-television movie, *The Canterville Ghost* (1996). Wanting to make the most of her first summer hiatus from *Party of Five*, Neve elected to star in the latest adaptation of Oscar Wilde's 1891 novella. The telefilm centers around a physics professor, Mr. Otis (Edward Wiley), who moves his family to England to take advantage of a research grant. Settling in the spooky and haunted Canterville Hall, the family encounters the resident specter, Sir Simon de Canterville (Patrick Stewart). Sir Simon is none too pleased with the Americans invading his home, and intends to scare them out of his family estate. Eventually, Sir Simon befriends the professor's daughter, Virginia (Neve), and the unlikely pair set out to rid him of his spiritual shackles.

To undertake the role of Virginia, Neve had to relocate to England for the shoot. The desire to visit Great Britain and work with Patrick Stewart of *Star Trek: The Next Generation* (1987–94) fame appealed to the young actress. "I'm starring in it with Patrick Stewart from *Star Trek*, who is actually one of my favorite actors, so that's gonna be a wonderful experience," Neve told *Tiger Beat*. "He plays a ghost and my character gets to save his soul."

The two-hour telefilm aired on January 27, 1996, to enthusiastic reviews. The *Hollywood Reporter* approved: "Stylish and engaging, *The Canterville Ghost* is a dashing good time." Neve was also heartily praised for her performance. A *USA Today* reviewer wrote, "As Virginia, a disgruntled teen unintimidated by the ghost's midnight chain-rattling, *Party of Five*'s soulful Neve Campbell is more than up to the challenge of sharing scenes with Stewart.... At the very least, it's refreshing to see a young Fox star like Campbell make such a charming fable instead of those horrible slash-&-stalk TV movies that the laughable *Melrose Place/90210* crowd is becoming so notorious for." *Canterville*

Ghost went on to earn a Family Film Award for Outstanding Television Movie from the World Film Institute, while Neve was honored with the Family Film Award for Outstanding Actress in a Television Movie.

An award, however, was not the only thing that Neve came away with from the *Canterville Ghost* experience. During filming, Neve decided to take the plunge and marry Jeff. Seeing that she had some free time in her schedule, Neve quickly warmed up to Jeff's proposition, which was at least partly motivated by his desire to get a green card. "I was doing a movie called *The Canterville Ghost* in England, and he was still living in Canada, and that was the time I had open," Neve explained matter-of-factly to *Rolling Stone* in September of 1997.

With Jeff beside her, Neve couldn't wait to start the next phase of her life. The separation, instead of diminishing her feelings for the thirty-year-old actor, had strengthened the couple's love. Never once questioning the degree of her commitment for Jeff, Campbell was sure she had found her soul mate. "Jeff is very generous and very understanding about my career—and he's incredibly funny," she said.

Neve prepared herself for the criticism she was sure would follow her decision to marry. "I know people are going to say I'm too young. But I feel confident," she expressed to *Soap Opera Digest*. "We've been together five years, and have put a lot of time and energy into this relationship."

Since Neve had often spoken out against the marital institution, the nuptials came as a complete surprise to her family. After surviving her parents' messy divorce, Campbell swore she would not marry young or enter lightly into any decision about a wedding. "I was twenty-one and had sworn I would never get married young because my parents did and it didn't work out," Neve told *Sassy*. "But then I realized that I had to look at my situation separately.... You either do it or you don't. I felt that if I wasn't willing to take the next step, why be in the relationship at all?"

Confident she was doing the right thing, Neve forged ahead with the wedding, planning a small, private affair with thirteen guests from the *Canterville* crew on April 4, 1995. The decision to exclude her relatives from the guest list was a difficult one for Neve. She loved each and every member of her family dearly, but was worried about the possible confrontations that would have threatened to ruin her special day. In the end, she decided that a private, spontaneous wedding would be better for all involved. "I always dreamed I would just have a small wedding because I wanted it to be my day," she confided to US magazine. "Unfortunately, a small wedding means immediate family, and my immediate family are all wonderful—but they're not all wonderful in the same room. So I thought it would be better and less political to just do it on my own. So I did, and we had an incredible day."

Marrying Jeff gave Neve the security she had been craving ever since she moved to Los Angeles. Everything was finally in place—love, career, and friendship. With her first television movie such a smashing success, Neve was quick to land another leading role, this time in the feature film *The Craft* (1996). She was flying high on life for the first time in years. "I jumped onto this roller coaster and it's going fast. But I think that because [acting] wasn't my dream my entire life, I'm not in a dream world," Neve revealed to *Soap Opera Digest* in January 1996. "I'm quite aware that things have happened quickly for me—and that they can stop as quickly as they started. But right now... I feel wonderful."

Seven

THE BIG PICTURE

ith a new husband and a new out-
look on life, Neve was all set to return to Los Angeles to begin work
on the second season (1995–96) of *Party of Five*. Before she could
do that, however, she had a honeymoon to enjoy and a new feature
film, *The Craft* (1996), to shoot. Traveling through Paris, Venice, and
Zurich with her new husband, Neve unwound from the pressures of the last year while taking in the sights and sounds of
Europe. After the three-week romantic getaway, it was right back
to Los Angeles, where Neve and Jeff had rented a two-bedroom
apartment in Brentwood, an upscale community adjacent to
Beverly Hills.

Although she hated to cut her honeymoon short, Campbell's
hopes of launching a career after *Party* required that she first
prove herself in big-screen movies. "When I did *The Craft* I was
simply looking to get into films. I couldn't then, or now, say, 'Okay,
I'm going to call [director Martin] Scorsese and see if he'll put me
in a film,'" she explained to *Mademoiselle*.

Columbia's *The Craft* follows the story of four young female
misfits attending a private school in Los Angeles, who use witchcraft to exact revenge on their high school tormentors. Initially,
the witchcraft serves to bring the young women closer together,

allowing them to cope with the difficulties of their social isolation. The sorceresses, however, turn against each other in the
violent, horrific climax. Playing the role of Bonnie, Neve starred
opposite actresses Fairuza Balk, Robin Tunney, and Rachel True,
all in their early twenties. "All of us are freaks at school. Bonnie
carries a dark secret. When she was a child she was in a fiery car
accident and burned very badly, and she was left with horrible
scars all over her body," Neve told *Extra*. "So she feels very insecure about herself and her body because of this trauma. The
other girls also have dark secrets which set them apart from the
other kids at school. We are misfits and don't fit in with everyone
else, but together we form our own clique."

Campbell had been reluctant to accept another project so
soon after completing *The Canterville Ghost*. Still recovering from
the draining experience, the prospect of doing another film right
away was hardly appealing to her, even though the movie was shot
in nearby California cities (Malibu, Los Angeles, and Tujunga). The
fact that she would have to star opposite three up-and-coming
actresses, who were all competing for the same spotlight, didn't help
matters any. "The truth is I didn't want to do the film at all because
I was really tired," she confided in *Sassy*, "...but the character
intrigued me."

Bonnie was a screen character Neve could really dig into.
Having endured her own share of early trauma, the actress
could relate to Bonnie's once-burned, twice-shy outlook on life.
Campbell was especially intrigued when she discovered that her
oncamera alter ego would go through a transformation much
like her own. "I think it was the fact that the role of Bonnie has
a huge transition in the film. She goes from being a real insecure 'freak type' who can't relate to anybody to becoming a very
strong, empowered young woman. Almost too confident," Neve
conveyed to *Venice* magazine. "To play transitions like that is a

wonderful thing because it's almost like you get to play two characters."

While Neve enjoyed depicting the evolution of Bonnie's character, she didn't care for the required daily makeover. The scars which Bonnie eventually eradicates through witchcraft were a daily hindrance to Neve. Working with the film's special effects crew, she was known to get frustrated with the trying process. "Man, the days that I had to wear those scars were such a nightmare," she complained to *Australian Hits*. "My days would be about eighteen hours long because I'd go in five hours before the rest of the crew to have my makeup put on. It isn't very good for the skin. It takes about an hour-and-a-half to take off because they have to slowly peel it away from your skin without ripping your skin."

The dark subject matter of the picture affected the atmosphere on the set. Skeptical from the beginning as to the viability of forming relationships with her female costars, Neve's worst fears regarding offcamera rivalry were confirmed. "We didn't really seem to click, and I don't know what the reason was for that," she revealed to *Rolling Stone*. "Rachel True and I became best friends, so that was good. But it was just four very different personalities. You just try to get through the day."

Adding to the mayhem of clashing egos was the witchery theme so cleverly explored by the director, Andrew Fleming (*Threesome, Bad Dreams*). In order to give the movie an authentic look and feel, a wicca (a neo-pagan religion) consultant was hired to advise the actors and director. Members of the cast were also given books on witchcraft to study between takes. For Neve, learning about the craft and laying some of her own superstitions to rest were highlights of working on the film. "We were all sent books on witchcraft," she told *Australian Hits*. "There's nothing to be afraid of. What I learned about witchcraft is that it's about strength within your own soul and it's the powers of nature—earth, air, water and fire. It's not really about evil. Black witchcraft can be about evil. But there's other witchcrafts."

While Neve had settled her fears and prejudices about wicca, several hair-raising experiences almost convinced her otherwise. It seemed that a coven of witches had become displeased with the manner in which the movie was portraying witchcraft. Naturally, they cursed the film. "We had this woman, Pat Devon, who was an actual witch, working with us on the set and she told us that there was an entire coven of witches who had put a curse on the movie because they were upset we might commercialize witch-craft or put it in a wrong light," Neve recounted to *Australian TV Week*. "Whether you believe in that or not, it's a scary thing in itself to be told. And there were a couple of occurrences in the film that you could say were either coincidence[s] or very odd situations."

One strange incident occurred during a plot sequence in which all four women were chanting an incantation in a forest. Hundreds of butterflies were supposed to magically appear around the young actresses. One butterfly, however, hovered in the mid-dle of the circle, as if stuck there, for the entire scene. An even more bizarre situation took place when the four actresses were standing in a formation around a circle of burning candles during a critical sequence set on the beach. "It was the middle of the night and it had taken hours to set up this scene and get the fire going and when the director said, 'Action,' the tide came up and put the fire out and swept all our candles down the beach," Camp-bell told *Australian TV Week*. "Then suddenly these bats came out of nowhere and flew overhead, which was frightening. The whole thing was really creepy."

Luckily for Columbia Pictures, the production team, and the actors, the "evil spell" lifted in time for the movie's debut on May 3, 1996. During its first week in release, *The Craft* earned an impressive $6.7 million at the box office, beating out Sharon

Stone's *Last Dance*, David Schwimmer and Gwyneth Paltrow's *The Pallbearer*, and Pamela Anderson Lee's *Barb Wire*. Because *The Craft* had a limited marketing budget, executives at Columbia Pictures did not expect it to score as high as it did. Jeff Blake, head of Sony Pictures/Columbia's distribution, told the *Los Angeles Times*: "The teenagers loved it because it was their movie and young women went for it because the sub-theme is about women taking control." Even Campbell quickly forgot the spooky time she had while working on the project, telling *Genre* in May 1996, "It was a good experience because it really is about four girls becoming empowered."

With its potent message of girl-power and a clever script, the film found favor with even the more skeptical of critics. A reporter for the *Dallas Morning News* said, "*The Craft* was a better flick than anyone had a right to expect, and Ms. Campbell was definitely noticed." The *Hollywood Reporter* also contributed a positive review, writing, "A modern day tale of a quartet of teenage witches who use their collective powers to exact vengeance on insensitive schoolmates and family members, the picture deftly combines sharp, knowing adolescent dialogue performed by a winning ensemble and effectively eerie scare tactics." Praising the actresses' performances, *Newsday* chimed in, "It must be said that *The Craft* is well made with a hard-driving pace. It places heavy demands on its four lead actresses, who come through in impressive fashion."

During its sixteen weeks in release, *The Craft* earned $24.7 million dollars in the U.S. and $30.9 million in ticket sales overseas. Appearing in a widely talked about box-office success, Neve had turned a pivotal corner in her career. Whereas before she was forced to chase down parts in films, thanks to *The Craft*'s success she would now be in control of her professional destiny. And while she had yet to prove that she could single-handedly carry a big-screen production, as she would later do with *Scream* (1996), Campbell was well on her way to becoming a powerful force in both television and film.

It was the summer of 1996, and Neve's domestic life was as fulfilling as her career. She and Jeff were still deeply entrenched in their blissful honeymoon phase and were busy discovering each other all over again. The cramped two-bedroom apartment they had been sharing suddenly felt too stifling, and the happy couple decided to look for a house. Her work on *The Canterville Ghost, Party of Five,* and *The Craft* allowed Neve to accumulate enough money for a spacious family home. There, Neve could stretch out in the dance studio she was already planning to build. After looking at just ten possible homes, the pair selected a gracious three-bedroom house nestled amid the verdure of chic Laurel Canyon. They didn't waste any time moving in. "I am married and it's just great. Things in my real life couldn't be better. I just moved into my first house with Jeff and we're very, very excited," she told *Detour*. "It's in the Hollywood Hills.... All of a sudden I'm obsessed about houses and furniture. I walk around the *Party of Five* set, thinking, 'That's a nice table.'"

A dance studio was just one of the many perks of living in her own house. The house came equipped with a full-size swimming pool, a luxury that she didn't take for granted. "Ever since I was a kid I had wanted a pool," she told *Detour*. Running from the pool to her own private dance studio, the actress couldn't believe that she was the proud owner of a home. At only twenty-one years of age, she was already living the Hollywood dream, and if it was all just a dream, she desperately hoped she would never wake up.

One night, however, Campbell awakened after sensing what she believed to be the presence of a young woman's ghost. Concluding that her new house was haunted, Neve dubbed her resident specter Madame X. The story got even more interesting when she discovered that a twenty-two-year-old maid had been brutally murdered in the house in 1991. The domestic was working for a mystery writer when a delivery man entered the home and committed the crime. Years later, the furnace in Campbell's house would turn off and on by itself and the lights would dim of their own accord. Unwilling to be frightened out of her new home, Neve made friends with the spirit, much as her character in *The Canterville Ghost* had befriended Simon de Canterville. She now considers the specter one of the family. "She's cool. I'm cool. We don't bug each other, so it's all right," she confirmed to *Detour* in March 1998.

The same could have been said of her relationship with Jeff. Prior to Jeff's arrival in the summer of 1995, Los Angeles had been a very lonely place for the actress, and she was not about to take his presence for granted. However, even she had to admit that life with Jeff was not always perfect. It wasn't surprising that with Neve's career skyrocketing and Jeff's stagnating, tension would erupt in the household. Though working steadily to meet casting directors, Jeff just couldn't catch a break in the ultra-competitive city. Watching Neve's career soar as he struggled to make a name for himself couldn't have been easy for the proud young man. To keep himself occupied, Jeff turned to writing. "He wrote a musical called *Starstruck* that was produced in Toronto a couple years ago," Neve reported to *Rolling Stone*. "And now he's gonna try and take it to New York and workshop it there."

It soon became very hard for Campbell to balance her relationship with the demands of her job. Hinting at her early marital frustrations, Neve said to *Cosmopolitan* magazine in January 1997, "Obviously, there are difficulties. The most important thing is to communicate, talk it out, and you'll be okay."

Whereas professional competition was putting a strain on their daily interaction, her long hours on the TV series set had begun to curtail even those brief moments together. Devoting fifteen hours daily to *Party of Five* didn't leave Neve much time to tend to her husband's needs. Since he had always been supportive of her career, urging her to go even further, she hoped he would be understanding during this particularly stressful time. "She's able to do everything," Colt explained to *People*, "so she wants to do it all."

That career drive, however, came with a high price. Neve barely had enough time to change and stumble into bed each night before falling into a deep sleep. When she did have time off, she escaped to her dance studio to ease the tension of her workday. "So, when I'm tired and need my own space, I spend time down there, I love that," she told *Australian Hits*.

The trouble brewing in Neve's paradise was so subtle that she failed to address the issues that would finally tear her marriage apart. But who could blame Neve for not guessing what the future would bring? A life this generally satisfying didn't seem needful of analyzing. Campbell decided to concentrate on the present rather than waste time worrying about any potential disasters.

Toward the end of her second season (1995–96) on *Party of Five*, Neve found herself yearning to make an even bigger impact on the big screen. The success of her first starring feature-film role in *The Craft* motivated her to pursue additional screen projects that would allow her to explore new characters and further develop as an actress. With the powerful agent Brandt Joel of Creative Artists Agency in Beverly Hills representing her since 1994, Neve was beginning to receive more scripts. It was tempting to think of switching gears. She was already growing tired of the routine of playing Julia every day. Even her *Party of Five* costars began to notice Neve's marked lack of enthusiasm for her role. Jeremy London, who plays Neve's onscreen husband, Griffin, told *Rolling Stone*, "I sometimes think she'd rather be doing her movies. Sometimes you get the impression that she's not really happy to be there."

The constant need to stretch her acting muscles was intrinsic to Neve's personality. It was precisely this desire to challenge herself and evolve into a better person, as evidenced by her struggle with the *Catwalk* producers back in Canada, that had helped her to defy the artistic and personal odds stacked against her. Another factor that contributed to her desire to change mediums was the time constraint that working on a weekly TV show presented. "Being on a series is hard because it takes a lot longer to get through to the end of the season. You're aware that you've got nine months to go when you start. And the hours tend to be somewhat longer," she revealed to *Australian Hits*. "Movies I love because you get to do different characters and eventually that's where I hope to go—strictly feature films. At that point, I'll have more time off, I'll be able to choose my films and characters, and feel somewhat more creative because I'll be able to play different characters."

Although she was beginning to get creatively restless, many aspects of the show were positive enough to warrant her ongoing commitment to *Party of Five*. After all, the TV series had given her the professional opportunities she has today. "It becomes tedious when you work fourteen hours a day playing the same character, with the same people," she revealed to *Total TV*. "Yet I love the people—they're my saving grace. And the writers are fantastic. So the show's been a good thing for me, and it's definitely springboarded my career into bigger and better things."

To make the most of her second hiatus from the show in the summer of 1996, Campbell signed on to star in a made-for-television film for the ABC network. These plans, however, were put on hold when she was given the opportunity to appear in *Scream*, a new film by Wes Craven, director of the horror classic *A Nightmare on Elm Street* (1984). Initially titled *Wes Craven's Scary Movie*, the theatrical feature took precedence, for Neve, over any telefeature. The top-notch cast included Courteney Cox, the thirty-two-year-old star of *Friends* (1994-present), and Skeet Ulrich, Neve's costar from *The Craft*. When Campbell informed the ABC executives that she was interested in pursuing another project, they graciously allowed her to bow out of her responsibilities, in exchange for a guarantee that she would later produce and star in an ABC network movie of her choice.

When it was time for Neve to select a project for ABC, she was immediately drawn to making a movie about Tourette Syndrome. Ever since her younger half-brother Damian had been diagnosed with the genetic neurological disorder, Neve has been using her celebrity status to raise public awareness about this debilitating illness. As the spokesperson for the Tourette Syndrome Association, she has been helping the organization raise money for research. So when the opportunity to reach a wide audience presented itself, Neve didn't hesitate to act. Unfortunately, ABC was not as supportive as she had hoped. They decided to pass on the project. Unwilling to be thwarted by the network's lukewarm reaction, she continues to speak out on behalf of the Tourette Syndrome Association.

Putting her plans to produce on hold, Campbell threw herself into making *Scream*, a film that would ultimately become the highest-grossing Hollywood thriller to date. While Neve had proved her star power in *The Craft*, she was by no means a shoo-in for the leading role of Sidney Prescott. Neve beat out stiff competition in the process. "I did two auditions and then I did a screen test," Neve told the *Mr. Showbiz* Web site. "It was down to two people. I always have a hard time just being cast in something [without auditioning], only because I love the concept of auditioning, of going in and having the challenge of being able to impress and win the role."

Before Neve came aboard, twenty-one-year-old Drew Barrymore (*Ever After, Never Been Kissed*) had signed on to play the role of Sidney. When another movie project interfered with her schedule, Barrymore relinquished the role. Not wanting to disappoint Craven and his crew, however, Drew agreed to play Casey Becker, who is killed in the first scene.

During the audition process, Neve's instincts about the role were right on the mark. Ironically, it was her first screen performance—in the "B" horror flick *The Dark* (1994)—that ultimately gave her the insight she needed to deliver the goods for *Scream*. "I think, with horror films, [the director] has to be very cautious and find actors that are going to be able to play the characters in a realistic way so that the film doesn't become a 'B' movie," she relayed to the *Mr. Showbiz* Web site. "In a scary film, you're already dealing with extreme circumstances; if it's not played in a realistic way, with some kind of heart, then the film is going to end up being bad quality."

Judging from the reactions of the director, producers, and casting directors, Neve was born to portray Sidney Prescott. With so many of the actresses who auditioned for the part reading the dialogue in an over-the-top manner, Neve's realistic, subtle, and sardonic approach stood out from the crowd. "The whole film depended on her. We agonized over who to cast because her role was instrumental," Craven told *People*. "But ultimately she was the linchpin without whom the movie wouldn't work. She's very wry and witty."

Cathy Konrad, the producer of *Scream*, also believed Campbell to be the perfect choice for the central role. Still a relative newcomer in Hollywood, the actress had just enough experience to carry a motion picture without detracting from the film's ensemble and its story. "We saw a lot of girls, but [it] had the stigma of being a horror movie," Konrad told the *Los Angeles Times*. "It prevented us from getting to a lot of actresses with a brand name for roles—a lot of agents didn't want to put their actresses in, quote, 'that kind of movie.' So we looked at a lot of new, fresh faces, and we came in contact with Neve. She's incredibly soulful; there's a lot going on below the surface. She has such good energy and she's so normal and identifiable as the girl next door."

Campbell's initial decision to headline in *Scream* had very little to do with her affinity for horror films. On the contrary, she'd never been a fan of the genre, and would often cringe in her seat with her eyes clenched shut while watching with friends. "I've seen very few scary movies, only because I have a real hard time sitting down for two hours and terrifying myself," she told the *Mr. Showbiz* Web site. "I end up being one of those people who holds a pillow in front of their faces and screams and cries a whole lot and then has nightmares for the next few months. But on a sleep-over with a friend when I was a kid, we watched *The Changeling* [1979]. It's a terrifying movie. The reason it scared me so much is that I do believe in spirits and ghosts, and that movie was about reincarnation and spirits. I took it too seriously."

Ultimately, what drew the actress to *Scream* had more to do with her fear of fright pictures than her appreciation of them. Just as *The Craft* had alleviated her fears of witchcraft, *Scream* provided a way for Neve to lessen her aversion to scary movies. "I've gotten to a place, actually, because of this film, where I can go back and watch those films and go, 'Oh, I get it,' " she explained to *Star Watch*. "It makes me appreciate the film all the more."

Scream's intelligent, mocking attitude toward slasher conventions and techniques showed a lighter side of thrillers that was a refreshing change. The parody of the thriller genre insisted that there was nothing to fear, so long as one avoids running upstairs while being chased by a killer, or saying, "I'll be right back" before leaving a room. "I loved the fact that it makes fun of the horror genre within the film," she revealed to *Australian TV Hits*. "People have been saying they love the fact that it's just as funny as it is scary. So, people that wouldn't normally get to a horror film are surprised and enjoyed it."

Her only hesitation was doing another thriller on the heels of *The Craft*. Not wanting to be typecast as a scream queen, like Jamie Lee Curtis had been in the late 1970s and early 1980s, Neve deliberated about accepting the offer. Would she be able to rise above the stereotype or be destined to play victims for the rest of her professional life? "That was definitely a big concern of mine even taking *Scream*, because I'd done *The Craft*. But on the other hand, *Scream* plays a different angle in the genre," she debated during a *Mr. Showbiz* interview.

Neve's attraction to good writing and tough female protagonists finally tipped the scales in favor of playing Sidney Prescott. The role was just too interesting to pass up. In a *Total TV* interview, she conveyed her view of the screen character. "She goes from being tormented, traumatized and insecure to being an overwhelmingly empowered and a strong young woman. And she grows up. In any film you get, you hope to have a transition like that. Besides, playing the lead in a studio feature is not a bad thing for a career."

Neve accepted the role and the many sleepless nights that would come with it. Wes Craven was pleased with her decision, telling the *Los Angeles Times* that she was perfect for the part in every way. "She was on it pretty fast, like a goose on a June bug. She wanted to play something different, just like Courteney Cox. She's been a dancer all her life, so she was able to be very physical and was able to control her body within the frame in a way that's quite unique. And from what I've seen on *Party of Five*, that show can be pretty lachrymose, and since this required a lot of crying, she had superb control of that."

Eight

SCREAMING INTO FAME

efore there was *Scream* the phenomenon, there was an out-of-work writer named Kevin Williamson. Born in New Bern, North Carolina, in 1965, the East Carolina University student of theater and film harbored ambitions of becoming the next Steven Spielberg. After a stint in New York City, Williamson relocated to Los Angeles in order to seriously pursue his career in film. After landing a day job as an assistant to a music video director, Williamson reserved his nights for brainstorming new stories and writing scripts.

The script *Killing Mrs. Tingle*, written in 1995, brought Williamson the break he thought would lead to bigger and better things. The celebration, however, was short-lived. "I had no money, I had no food, my phone bill was due," he recalled during a December 1999 *Sci-Fi Universe* interview. "I had written the movie, *Killing Mrs. Tingle*, which I had optioned off to Interscope, and gotten enough money to pay off my college loans, my car payment, and all the people I had borrowed money from the last ten years. [Then the project went into turnaround, not to be made as a film for several years.] I had nothing left, I was broke again."

In the nick of time and in the span of one weekend, Kevin hatched a brilliant idea for a new film he called *Scary Movie*. The concept, he confirmed to *Entertainment Weekly*, was inspired by "watching a Barbara Walters special on the Gainesville [Florida] murders. I was broke, house-sitting for a friend to pay him back for money he'd lent me for groceries, and I was scaring the hell out of myself. I thought I heard a noise. I walked the house with a butcher knife and a phone, and called a friend while I searched the place. We got into this huge discussion, testing each other on horror movies. And that's how *Scream* was born."

During that fateful evening, Williamson crafted the now-famous opening scene in which the young and attractive Casey Becker (Drew Barrymore) is confronted by a serial killer just as she is preparing to pop a horror film into the VCR. A draft of the sequence lingered in Williamson's drawer until a few weeks later, when he decided to finish it once and for all. As a last ditch effort for success and recognition, Williamson holed up in a Palm Springs hotel room and stayed put for three days until he had a completed screenplay in his hands.

The plot of *Scream* opens in the fictitious town of Woodsboro, California, one year after the brutal death of Sidney Prescott's mother. With the killer still on the loose and an innocent man imprisoned for the crime, Sidney still harbors doubts about her mother's death. After the murder of Sidney's classmate, Casey, it is discovered that someone wearing a mask inspired by Edvard Munch's painting *The Scream* is killing teenagers. The narrative concludes with Sidney discovering that the killers are none other than her boyfriend, Billy (Skeet Ulrich), and his movie trivia–obsessed friend Stu (Matthew Lillard).

A fan of gory thrillers, Williamson could recite almost every line ever uttered in a genre film entry. This knowledge, coupled with a scathing wit, resulted in a Hollywood horror flick unlike any other ever made. A seasoned critic of the horror species, he grew up in a time when slasher entries like *Halloween* (1978), *Friday the*

13th (1980), and *Prom Night* (1980) were dominating movie theaters. Williamson longed to resuscitate the lost art while abolishing its tired conventions. "My intention was just to make a scary movie. I wanted to be scared," he informed *Sci-Fi Universe*. "I thought we hadn't had a scary movie in a really, really long time. Horror movies had just become so predictable and plot-driven. The characters were always these stick-figures that really didn't amount to anything. The characters' sole purpose in the script was just to push the plot from point A to point B and back. So I kind of thought, well, what if we had sort of a scary movie with a little touch of Agatha Christie in there?"

The masterpiece completed, Williamson wasted no time sending it to his agent. If nothing else, he hoped the screenplay could be used as a writing sample in his efforts to secure work as a writer for teen-related TV shows. "I gave the draft to my agent, and he went through the roof. He sent it out immediately but I thought it would never sell," recalled Williamson. "Horror movies have never really done well on the spec market. After the first day, no one had made an offer. New Line [Cinema] passed and I thought the script was dead in the water."

It took several days, but eventually there was only one word out on the industry street: *Buy! Buy! Buy!* What had been written in just one weekend had suddenly become the hottest intellectual property in town, with Miramax, Paramount, Oliver Stone, Morgan Creek, and many other film companies trying to outbid one another. Because they promised an early release, Williamson eventually sold his script to Miramax's horror film division, Dimension Films.

The decision to place his screenplay with Dimension came after a conversation between Williamson and his lawyer, Pattie Felker. Because production of *Killing Mrs. Tingle* had been held up for nearly two years, Felker urged Kevin to sign with the company that was not only offering the highest bid, but whose executives were committed to releasing the film in a timely manner. "Bob Weinstein, owner, co-chairman, head of Miramax, had loved the script," Williamson explained. "He had just opened a new division called Dimension Films which was dedicated to this type of movie, and had promised to make this film right away. And getting a movie made was a hell of a lot more important than the money. I really wanted to see *Scary Movie* made, so Bob and Dimension got the script."

No sooner had Dimension Films made the acquisition than Wes Craven was approached to direct the project. Known as the "master of horror," Craven made his film debut with the seminal thrillers *Last House on the Left* (1972) and *The Hills Have Eyes* (1977). But it wasn't until the commercial success of *A Nightmare on Elm Street* (1984) that Craven finally gained a mainstream following. Although Wes Craven established the hugely popular *Nightmare* franchise, he left the property after the original. For the next ten years, Craven directed several lesser-known movies, including *Swamp Thing* (1982), *The Serpent and the Rainbow* (1988), *Shocker* (1989), and *The People Under the Stairs* (1992). In the late 1980s, he contributed to several episodes of the revived *The Twilight Zone* (1985–88) TV series. "Wes Craven in many ways was the perfect choice for this movie. He knew these movies inside and out and I think, quite frankly, he was tired of them," said Williamson. "I think he saw *Scream* as a challenge. He understood what I had set out to do with the horror genre and he completely concurred. He loved the idea of exposing the conventions of the genre. Wes gave *Scary Movie* its tone. He brought it to life with a perverse wickedness and I'm forever grateful."

Craven was reluctant to accept the offer to direct *Scream*. He had been looking for something fresh to put his cinematic signature on. Unfortunately, most of the films he was being offered didn't measure up to his standards. Even before reading Williamson's script, he told *Entertainment Weekly*, "People have asked for years if horror movies can make a comeback. They can as long as they're good. But lately, they haven't been."

After giving the Williamson script a cursory glance, Craven knew he had a winner on his hands. He appreciated the writer's incorporation of a new horror paradigm, where technology could be used as a tool of destruction. He explained to the *Los Angeles Daily News*, "The telephone is the edged weapon of technology. You can reach straight into the heart of a locked-up house, and suddenly there is someone personally with you. The killer can be calling you from right outside your window, whereas once they'd have to have been in a phone booth."

When the script had reached Craven, he was busy working on a remake of the 1963 thriller *The Haunting* (a project later taken over by director Jan De Bont). He had only recently begun toying with the idea of reaching a wider audience than the usual genre fans. *Scream* promised to do that and much more. "It doesn't treat the audience like idiots," Craven observed to the *New York Times*. "It's very strange. The genre is deteriorating, but the scariest films confront our very real primal fears. And there's something about the bluntness of this movie, the unadorned truth of it, that flies in the face of so many movies where every truth is massaged and prettified to be nonthreatening." Clearly, Craven was raring to take American audiences on a ride they would not soon forget.

In the spring of 1995, *Scream* was set to begin shooting in Santa Rosa, California (fifty-two miles north of San Francisco), but when local residents objected to the use of the town's high school because of the graphic and violent content of the film, production was moved to Healdsburg, California (eleven miles north of Santa Rosa). A talented group of actors, including Drew Barrymore,

David Arquette (*Beautiful Girls, Johns*), Skeet Ulrich (*The Craft, Boys*), Courteney Cox (TV's *Friends*), Matthew Lillard (*Mad Love, Hackers*), and Liev Schreiber (*Ransom, The Daytrippers*) had signed on to play opposite Neve, and the group was soon screaming the night away during the late evening shoots.

Coming off the second harmonious *Party of Five* season, Neve hoped that her new big-screen coworkers would be just as amicable. Upon meeting the cast, Campbell realized she would have nothing to worry about. "I got along with everybody on the set. I think we're all finding strengths in our differences," she told *Femme Fatales*. "We're all learning from each other, not only in life but within the film as well. The crew is one of the best. I get so worried about starting a film because, if you've ever been on a really tough set, you know what that's like and God forbid if you have to work for three months straight and have a miserable time. If there's just one bad apple, that will ruin it for everyone."

In place of the backstabbing rivalry she had encountered on past shoots, Campbell found herself in the company of a supportive group of actors. The cast's mutual respect for one another was evidenced by Cox's description of Neve in a *TV Guide* interview: "She had an extremely hard part in this movie, to be on the verge of fright and tears throughout and to keep it so interesting and real at the same time. She could do it because she's grounded. She's a centered human being."

The atmosphere on the *Scream* set was one of fun and invention. Because the movie was about breaking horror conventions and trying something new, the actors were given the freedom to improvise and experiment. Neve elaborated on this freedom in an interview: "What I'm really excited about is that each actor in the movie has taken their character to another level, and added things to the performance that aren't on the page. We have been fairly consistent in following the script, so we usually just make little line changes; however, if the emotion has risen to a higher level, you can improvise and add those emotions to the scenes. We're given the time and opportunity to do that."

Even more appealing to Neve were the physical challenges of the role. Almost five years had passed since her days as a professional dancer, and she missed pushing her body to its limits. Consequently, she welcomed the opportunity to perform some of her own stunts. "I loved doing action. You know, it's funny, before I did *Scream*, I had said, 'Oh, I'll never do an action film.' Because, you know, a lot of times there's not a lot of depth to the characters," Neve revealed to *TV Guide*. "But after I did *Scream*, I was really psyched about being able to fight and punch and do stunt work. I think a lot of that comes from being physically active, because I'm a dancer, so anything physical on the set that's challenging is a lot of fun for me and that's what I enjoyed."

The day Neve's character was supposed to punch Courteney Cox's Gale Weathers was one of the most memorable for the actress. Campbell had never slugged anyone before, and got a little carried away during her first run-through with Cox. In an interview with late night TV talk show host Conan O'Brien, Neve recalled, "The first day that Courteney and I worked together, I walked up to her, I was really excited about working with her. And I walk up and go, 'You know what, I'm so excited, I get to punch you today!' And I walked away, and I was like, 'Oh, Gee, I don't know if she took that right.' So I went back and I apologized."

It was obvious that Neve had been away from the dance studio too long: Her overzealous desire to perform stunts and other physical activities was always apparent. Craven loved the spirit and bravery with which Campbell approached even the most daunting of action sequences, but he wasn't about to take chances with her safety. Some of the more dangerous stunt work had been reserved for professionals, but Neve couldn't resist asking to do the stunts herself. She told the *Toronto Sun*, "I was begging Wes to let me do more stunts, but he wouldn't let me."

Neve and the director may not have seen eye to eye in the stunt department, but they were compatible in almost every other respect. Craven's directorial vision inspired Campbell to achieve more than she thought herself capable of. He had a deep respect for the young actress's intense work ethic. Amazed with her powers of concentration, he told the *Los Angeles Times* that "she knows where her character is at every moment, which is one of the chief challenges of shooting out of sequence. She remembers at what level of intensity her character was when we shot four weeks ago. Neve just hits it, she stays in character all day, even at an especially intense level. Many actors float away from it, and it's difficult to keep them in place. They'll go goof off or go take a nap. But Neve, at the first take, is always up to speed."

Having worked with a fair share of directors in her life, Neve was able to appreciate Craven's contribution. His assistance proved invaluable to her professional development. It was during the making of *Scream* that she discovered the power of visualization in bringing her performance to life. "He's really able to create images that bring you to where you need to be within a dramatic scene," she told *Femme Fatale*. "I was doing a scene the other day, we had one last take and Wes said to me, 'Okay, you've got a thousand bullets ringing through your body, now go do it.' That helped me so much. Wes really has this incredible sort of insight into what an actor needs, so I really loved working with him."

All the help in the world, however, couldn't save her from the special effects that were a vital part of the production. One of the most unpleasant aspects of working on *Scream* was having to be covered with blood on a daily basis. "I was constantly getting slashed at certain points in the movie, or people were getting slashed in front of me and we'd have to have [the] continuity of other people's blood on me," she recounted to the *Los Angeles Times*. "It got a little ridiculous. You pretty much have three or four people attacking you with blood daily, which is a pretty interesting experience. I've done some pretty bloody stuff on Halloween, but I've never been that bloody. On the last day of shooting, I was so sick of wearing the wardrobe. Because they wanted to keep the continuity on the wardrobe, they stopped washing it. So, for the last three weeks of shooting the last scene of the movie, I would go in and put on the clothes, and they'd be like cardboard. They'd be so hard, and they'd wet them down again with water and add some more blood. On the last day, I took a paintbrush of blood to a lot of people on the crew, to get back at everyone."

Practical jokes aside, Neve's experience on the *Scream* set was not all fun and games. Whereas during the first few weeks she had been able to complete the night shoots with no apparent difficulties, her endurance was stretched to its limits when the 1996–97 *Party of Five* season began filming. Working exclusively on *Scream* had been one of the best times of her life, but moonlighting for the film was beginning to take a toll on her well-being. Sleep had become a luxury she just couldn't afford. "I would finish at six in the morning on *Scream*, get home at 6:30, have 15 minutes to shower and get in the car for *Party of Five* and work all day," Neve informed *Twist*.

A lesser person might have folded under such pressure. Yet Neve survived the ordeal by stealing catnaps in her trailer whenever the chance arose. "You're actually better off not even questioning the length of time you have to not have a break," she told the *Los Angeles Times*. "You have to learn to lie down when you have time to lie down, and how to save your energy and spend it when you have to."

Craven watched as Neve struggled to keep herself awake during the all-night shoots. Struck by her endurance and consummate professionalism, he conveyed to *USA Weekend*, "I think because she's done theatre, she just knows the concept of 'the show must go on' and the person is less important than the whole. I have no illusion that she doesn't have pain. That's part of what makes her so interesting."

For Neve, realizing the boundaries of her endurance would prove to be dangerous. She would eventually find herself in the precarious position of trying to do it all. At the time, however, her main goal was to compile an impressive body of screen work to back her up after *Party of Five* ended its run. "I'm tired," she confessed to *People*. "But it's necessary to get my face out there." Her career depended on it.

Veterans like Cathy Konrad, producer of *Scream*, told Neve that she was right. "Neve has a step up because audiences have been identifying with her for years on *Party of Five*," Konrad explained to *Time International*. "When she makes her real star turn, she'll have a body of work behind her."

With similar encouragement from her friends, agent, and coworkers, Campbell wasn't about to question her decision to sacrifice her personal life for her career. Career opportunities like Neve's don't come along every day, and the importance of not wasting this rare chance at stardom was not lost on her. What escaped her attention was the need to balance her life properly. It would take a long time for her to figure out how to relax, enjoy her success, and still win the Hollywood race. In the meantime, she desperately missed the simpler days of her youth when she could just act her age by kicking back with close friends and family members. "I would like to sleep more. I would like to have more of a life," she confessed to *E! Online* in December 1997. "I would like to have stronger relationships with the people I love. I would like to have conversations that have nothing to do with the Industry. Picnics on Center Island in Toronto, with some friends, a bucket of Kentucky Fried Chicken, a beer and a Frisbee. Good conversations and relating to people. Those are the most important things to me in my life."

Her initiation into the entertainment industry complete, Neve was about to enter a new stage of her hectic life. The next phase would entail more conflict and struggle then she had ever anticipated. Fame for its own sake did not interest her, money was just a by-product of success, and the esteem of her peers didn't mean half as much as the performer's opinion of herself. So what was it that was driving the twenty-three-year-old actress to forsake her privacy, relationships, and personal time? Answering that question requires that one trace back to her childhood, to a time when she craved the acceptance of her peers and loathed herself for wanting it; when she wished for her parents' reconciliation, but hated the idea of living in the same house with the two of them constantly arguing.

Neve's contradictory needs—for love and solitude, fame and privacy, luxury and simplicity—were about to dredge up the past she thought she had finally escaped. Of course, she could always fall back on the one coping strategy that had never failed her when times got tough—to simply get up, brush herself off, and start all over again. "I really don't believe that anything is negative," she told *USA Weekly*. "Any kind of experience, whether it seems to be negative or positive, if you learn from it and you grow from it and you are aware of where you are within it, then you've made it positive somehow."

Nine

WILD AT HEART

he release of *Scream* was a monumental event in the history of Hollywood horror films. Opening on December 20, 1996, during a holiday weekend, the picture beat out such blockbusters as director Tim Burton's *Mars Attacks!* with Jack Nicholson and the romantic comedy *One Fine Day* starring Michelle Pfeiffer and George Clooney. Boasting a slim $14 million production budget and a $25 million marketing campaign, *Scream* grossed an amazing $103 million domestically and an additional $75 million overseas—all this before pay TV, home video, and DVD rentals and sales were added into the impressive computation.

Never before had a horror movie done so well at the box office. Before the *Scream* epoch, the highest-grossing fright-fests included *Pet Sematary* (1989) at $57.5 million, *A Nightmare on Elm Street 4: The Dream Master* (1988) at $49.4 million, and *Halloween* (1978) at $47 million. Fueled by the ever-growing teen demographic and its craving for horror, *Scream* had officially become a phenomenon. "Normally it's four weekends and you're gone," Bob Weinstein, Miramax films co-chairman, told *Entertainment Weekly*. "But this one stuck around for twenty-six weeks in wide release. It was almost frightening."

Figures are all well and good, but more conclusive evidence of *Scream*'s domination could be found in the copycat efforts of Hollywood studio executives. If imitation is truly the most sincere form of flattery, then the rash of follow-up movies, like *Urban Legend* (1998), *I Know What You Did Last Summer* (1997), and *Halloween H20* (1998), would prove that *Scream* had ushered in a new era of horror in Hollywood.

Young and old moviegoers alike seemingly could not get enough of *Scream*, making several return trips to the "scene of the crime." "People are seeing *Scream* five and six times," *Scream* producer Cary Wood explained to the *New York Times*. "It's become a communal experience. They're repeating lines from it."

Todd Doogan, creator of the movie-oriented Web site *Rough Cut*, agreed, telling *Newsday*, "It's become quite a phenomenon. A lot of teenybopper girls are wearing *Scream* T-shirts and shouting the lines of the movie before they are spoken onscreen. It makes them feel hip and smart."

No one was more surprised by the movie's triumphant box-office spree than the people who had made it all happen. Filmmaker Wes Craven hoped that *Scream* would be his comeback project, but he'd had some last minute doubts. Although he was proud of the final result, he could never have predicted the audience's reaction. "We went off to Christmas vacation last year thinking Beavis and Butthead [*Beavis and Butt-head Do America*, the animated feature film opened the same weekend] had kicked our butts," Craven conveyed to *Entertainment Weekly*. "We come back and *Scream* is all people are talking about."

Neve was totally surprised by the public's response. During the long shoot she hadn't given much thought to the picture's commercial viability. But, when the results were tabulated, she couldn't help but breathe a long sigh of relief. Her hard work and near exhaustion had paid off richly. "Obviously, when you work on a project you always hope it's going to do extremely well but I wasn't always sure how it would be received at the time," she gleefully reported to *Australian TV Hits*. "It seems that everyone was sort of looking for a horror film, so it was definitely a surprise."

Everyone had their own explanation for the movie's huge success. Convinced the film's high fear factor was responsible for its instant hit status, Courteney Cox offered her own take on the phenomenon sweeping the country. "I was in the movie and I still can't watch *Scream* all the way through," she explained to *Entertainment Weekly*. "I think that's what made it such a success."

Miramax executive Bob Weinstein provided another explanation, praising the film's outlandish mutation of a worn-out format. "*Scream* crosses every boundary. It's not just scary, it's not just fun, it's not just clever, it's not just a whodunit," he elaborated. "It's all that and it's something more. Like *The Crying Game* [1992] or *Pulp Fiction* [1994], the *Scream* saga's a whole new approach to movies. It kills off all the old formulas."

It's a rarity in Hollywood when teenagers and critics can agree on anything, but *Scream* shattered the boundaries separating the worlds of high art and blatant commercialism. Bob Strauss, a film critic for the *Los Angeles Daily News*, enthused, "*Scream* . . . stays visceral and amusing from beginning to end. It's the best acted, most suspenseful slasher movie in a month of *Friday the 13ths*. And the comic premise here is, indeed, a nonstop scream." A *Los Angeles Times* critic echoed that notion: "It's sensational in both senses of the word: a bravura, provocative send-up of horror pictures that's all scary and gruesome, yet too swift-moving to lapse into morbidity. It risks going way over the top, deliberately generating considerable laughter in the process."

All these accolades, however, were just the beginning. Neve earned the Academy of Science Fiction, Horror, and Fantasy Films' Saturn Award for Best Actress, and was nominated for an

MTV Movie Award for Best Female Performance, losing to Claire Danes for *William Shakespeare's Romeo and Juliet*. *Scream* won MTV's Best Movie Award and the Saturn Award for Best Horror Film in 1997.

As a result of this runaway movie hit, Neve Campbell had become one of the most sought-after young actresses in Hollywood, alongside such favorites as Drew Barrymore (*Boys on the Side*, *The Wedding Singer*), Claire Danes (*Home for the Holidays*, *My So-Called Life*), and Winona Ryder (*Edward Scissorhands*, *Little Women*). Studios weren't the only ones trying to get close to Neve. Fans who had never before seen an episode of *Party of Five* were tuning in to the TV series just to glimpse the breakout star of the year. In the months following *Scream*'s premiere, Campbell seemed to be on everyone's wish list for upcoming film projects. A *Rolling Stone* magazine cover (among many others), TV talk show appearances, a hosting stint on *Saturday Night Live* with musical guest David Bowie, and a spot in the famous milk "mustache" print ads were all testament to the enormous impact her performance had on the world. *Entertainment Weekly* now labeled Campbell "one of Hollywood's top Gen-X ingenues."

Back in Canada, Neve's parents, Marnie and Gerry, were surprised by their daughter's sudden rise to superstardom. Marnie started a fan club to help Neve sort through the thousands of fan letters she was receiving each month. Gerry was also supportive of Neve during this overwhelming period, offering his daughter words of wisdom about staying grounded in the midst of the promotional activity. Her brother Christian, who was still living in Los Angeles, felt Neve's sudden fame much more keenly, because it wasn't happening to him. Other than an eleven-episode run on producer Aaron Spelling's failed TV series *Malibu Shores* (1996), Christian had difficulty finding acting jobs. Though frustrated

The Salinger family at the Fox network party at New York City's Tavern on the Green in 1994. (© Kathy Hutchins/Hutchins Photo Agency)

Lacey Chabert and Neve pal around during the 1994 Fox party at Tavern on the Green.
(© Kathy Hutchins/Hutchins Photo Agency)

Caught off guard at the Hollywood Athletic Club in 1994, Neve makes the most of her photo op.
(© Kathy Hutchins/Hutchins Photo Agency)

Neve and Michael Goorjian take a break during the filming of "The Wedding" episode of *Party of Five*. (© Brenda Scott Royce)

Scott Wolf and Neve take a stroll on the Sony Pictures lot.
(© Brenda Scott Royce)

Neve Campbell as Julia Salinger on the second season of *Party of Five*.
(© Jeffrey Thurnher/Archive Photos)

Neve takes five in a comfy bathrobe.
(© Brenda Scott Royce)

All eyes are on Neve when she shows up for the *Scream* premiere in 1996.
(© Kathy Hutchins/Hutchins Photo Agency)

With fellow cast mate and friend Jennifer Love Hewitt backing her up, Neve makes an appearance at the 54th annual Golden Globe Awards in Janurary of 1997.
(© Kathy Hutchins/Hutchins Photo Agency)

Neve makes a wild entrance at the 1997 MTV Movie Awards held in June.
(© Kathy Hutchins/Hutchins Photo Agency)

Neve accepts the award for Outstanding Actress in a Television Film for her role in *The Canterville Ghost* during the Family Film Awards in August of 1996.
(© Reuters/Fred Prouser/Archive Photos)

Brother Christian supports Neve at the 1997 premiere of *Scream 2*.
(© Kathy Hutchins/Hutchins Photo Agency)

Neve smiles for the press at the 49th annual Emmy Awards in September of 1997.
(© Kathy Hutchins/Hutchins Photo Agency)

Neve and mother Marnie Campbell bond during a 1998 benefit for the Tourette's Syndrome Association.
(© Kathy Hutchins/Hutchins Photo Agency)

Neve shines at the *Vanity Fair* Oscar
Party in March 1998.
(© Kathy Hutchins/Hutchins Photo Agency)

Neve decides that less is more at the
1998 *Wild Things* premiere.
(© Kathy Hutchins/Hutchins Photo Agency)

Neve shows her support for breast
cancer research at Revlon's 1998 Fire
and Ice Ball.
(© Chris Moody/Hutchins Photo Agency)

Neve makes another appearance at
the *Vanity Fair* Oscars Party in 1999,
where she was seated next to Monica
Lewinsky.
(© Kathy Hutchins/Hutchins Photo Agency)

Neve shows off her 1998 Blockbuster Entertainment
Award after the presentation.
(© Kathy Hutchins/Hutchins Photo Agency)

Neve comes out to support her fellow actors in the
Jack Bull premiere in 1999.
(© Kathy Hutchins/Hutchins Photo Agency)

Neve strikes a pose with *Wild Things* costars Denise Richards and Kevin Bacon at the 1998 Blockbuster Entertainment Awards held in March.
(© Deidre Davidson/Saga/Archive Photos)

Neve comes out to celebrate the 100th episode of *Party of Five* in 1998.
(© Kathy Hutchins/Hutchins Photo Agency)

with his own slow progress, he tried to be supportive of his sister's success. Neve's husband, Jeff, was also battling with feelings of inferiority. His acting career had been at an impasse ever since he moved to the City of Angels in 1995. Seeing his wife's face on billboards and magazine covers couldn't have been easy.

Indeed, Neve was becoming a ubiquitous presence in the public eye. Her sudden popularity was so overwhelming that she had difficulty handling the fanatics and photojournalists that were trailing her around Los Angeles. The attention was getting so out of hand, she was even forced to disguise her appearance. "I have a blonde wig I wear when I go out. It works. No one recognizes me," she confessed to the Quincy, Massachusetts, newspaper *The Patriot Ledger.*

While playing hide-and-seek with the paparazzi, Neve quickly realized the importance of keeping her offcamera life private. In a revealing interview with *E! Online,* she rattled off a laundry list of newfound problems, complete with her own solution. "The press continues to review me. I can't really kick that," she explained. "The bad aspects obviously are loss of privacy and feeling as though people want to create a persona for you that isn't necessarily who you truly are. But on the other hand, if you handle it in the right way, you can also express who you truly are."

As most people in the public eye will attest, appearing in the pages of a supermarket tabloid is somewhat of a rites of passage. When the masses became hungry for all things Neve, these papers were quick to produce stories detailing the goings-on in her haunted house, as well as her alleged top-secret weight-loss strategy. Displaying a keen sense of humor, Neve joked with *Entertainment Asylum* (an online entertainment network) about the absurdity of tabloid reporting. "I think it was the [*National*] *Enquirer* or something like that a month ago, and they put in my

entire diet—from the kind of juice I drink to my favorite snack, which is frozen grapes," she explained. "I've never had frozen grapes in my life. A friend of mine tried it the other day, and said it was actually pretty good. Wow, I might try that. According to me, I love it. Kind of a little odd."

"Focusing on the positive had become second nature for Neve. Through most of her life, with every good thing that happened to her, something negative seemed not far behind. In order to keep from losing sight of her good fortune, twenty-three-year-old Neve concentrated on counting her many new blessings. This glass-half-full approach to life helped her in dealing with enthusiastic fans. Going so far as to accommodate them by screaming on command, Campbell showed her devotees that she had remained as accessible and as grounded as ever. "It happens all the time," she informed *People*. "I love screaming, so usually I do it. I like to cooperate. Plus, I've been screaming all my life. I learned how by doing *The Phantom of the Opera* as a kid. Believe me, we spent the whole play screaming."

Though instantly recognizable wherever she went, Neve didn't adopt the manner of a big-time celebrity. While most stars trade their massive earnings for huge mansions and fancy clothes, Campbell preferred the simple things to the status symbols she watched many of her contemporaries amassing.

Certainly, Neve's modest, working-class upbringing had a lot to do with her thrifty nature. The main reason, however, was that she had yet to come to grips with the idea of being rich and famous. The notion that she was one of the most popular rising stars of the late 1990s had not fully dawned upon the hard-working actress. Laboring so diligently to secure a place in the industry's hierarchy, she had almost forgotten to savor the fruits of her labor. It took the prodding of one of her friends to finally convince Neve to invest in her dream car. "I was driving around

with a friend one day and saw a Porsche and said, 'God, I'd love to have one of those,'" she confided to *Australian Hits*. "And my friend was like, 'You can.'"

As things stood, reflection on the tumultuous activity of the recent months was a luxury Neve could not afford. The actress had everything she could possibly want—fame, money, and a thriving career—everything except the one thing she longed for—solitude. And it was during those crazy days of *Scream* that Neve started feeling that she had lost something vital: an essential part of herself that she could never recover.

Slowly but surely she began to pull away from her husband, Jeff. She was no longer the shy, insecure girl who craved attention and love. A mature young woman, Neve had learned how to take care of herself. The place and time of their first meeting seemed like a phantom that had disappeared into the dark night.

The wonder of youth, first love, and innocence was something Campbell could never reclaim, even if she wished to. "Life seems very unrealistic and overwhelming in a lot of ways," she explained to *Detour* in March 1998. "And going back to remembering when I was a child, and I was someone's niece, and I was someone's sister, and I was someone's daughter, and when that's all I was, was just Neve—I felt a loss there. I can't go back. Not that I would choose to. But it makes me sad."

In mid-1997, Neve's already fragile world came crashing down around her. In a statement to the press dated July 29, 1997, she announced her separation from Jeff Colt, her husband of three years. "Jeff and I have been together for over six and a half years," she wrote. "We've been through a lot, and we've learned much from each other. However, we have come to realize that both of us have some growing to do, and we need to be on our own for a while. There has always been much more depth to our relationship than the press and public could see. Jeff and I love each other very much, and that's going to continue."

The public may have been surprised by this sudden disclosure, but those close to the rising star knew all too well that the separation and ensuing divorce had been long in the coming. Jeff and Neve's ten-year age difference had become a major obstacle to their happiness. When they first met, Neve was young and impressionable. She believed that theirs was a love that could bridge the generation gap. However, as she came into her own as a person, she found her wants, needs, and desires all subject to reevaluation. Jeff, however, was already in his early thirties, and the couple found themselves in the awkward position of having too little in common. She explained to *Mademoiselle*, "I look back and think, I thought I knew everything, and I knew nothing."

Some close sources hinted that professional rivalry was the main factor leading to the domestic breakup. Even Colt half-joked about his frustration in an interview with *People* magazine, saying, "People call me Mr. Campbell." But Neve denied the allegations that Jeff was somehow threatened by her professional triumphs. "Jeff is not jealous of my success, but he definitely wishes things would be more equal," she revealed to the *Calgary Sun* in December 1997. "It's frustrating as an actor not to be working to your potential. Jeff and I went on vacation to Greece to get away from the *Party* mania in Los Angeles only to discover it's worse in Greece. *Party* is a huge hit in Europe. No matter where we went, I'd get recognized."

Though she'd be the first to own up to not having spent enough time with her husband, Neve wouldn't accept all the blame for the failed relationship. Before she got married, she was very explicit about her realistic expectations. The young actress hoped that the love match would work, but she had been prepared for the separation that her parents' divorces had made seem inevitable. "If we grow apart," she told *People* magazine, "that's a circumstance we'll deal with."

Before the separation announcement was even released, Neve had made allusions to the problematic union. She had spent the better part of her marriage trying to put aside her growing concerns about the future. After repeatedly recounting the details of her blissful union to the media, Neve could not lie to herself any longer. The feelings she had had for Colt as a young girl were now a thing of the past, and although she loved him dearly as a friend, the honeymoon was definitely over. "Jeff and I both have a very realistic view of marriage," she explained to *TV Guide*. "You try as hard as you can, and you love each other as much as you can, and you hope to grow together. You hope that divorce is not an option. But if you're miserable, you know, together, then why continue?"

Whether the two had simply grown apart or were divided by the growing demands of Neve's flourishing career will never fully be ascertained. All Campbell knew was that she was beginning to feel suffocated by the man to whom she had once sworn undying love. Her marriage was not allowing her the freedom to change and evolve. "There's one passage about relationships," she conveyed to *Time International*, "about two trees growing, and if they grow too close together, they'll shade one another and won't be allowed to grow, but if they grow enough of a distance apart, they'll be able to grow and continue their love. I find that to be really beautiful."

Divorce seemed the only way Neve could reclaim her independence. The only hitch was, what would she do now? Neve had complained about the loneliness of living in Los Angeles on countless occasions. She had gotten accustomed to Jeff's presence, and began wondering if she could manage being on her own. Not the type to hop from one relationship to another in search of security, Campbell planned to take this opportunity to learn about the one person she had been neglecting the most—herself. "I deserve a healthy, healing time . . .'" Neve told *Mademoiselle*. "I need to take some time to see if I'm all right not being in a relationship."

After Jeff moved out of their home and the couple filed for divorce on November 6, 1997, the call of the "wild" beckoned Neve. Never having had the chance to let loose as a young girl, the liberty she felt after separating from Jeff Colt was a welcome relief. She was only twenty-three, and already wise well beyond her years. Understandably tired of always playing the good girl and doing the right thing, Campbell made a career choice that had more to do with her new state of mind than any professional consideration. She may as well have been talking about the reason behind her emancipation from Jeff when she explained why she had decided to portray hard-as-nails Suzie Toller in the sexy thriller *Wild Things* (1998): "I think it's important to try out different kinds of roles as early in your career as possible," Neve told the Ireland Film and Television network. "When you get older, people are less likely to accept you in anything new. I'm keen to take a shot at as many styles and characters as possible right now, even if it's just to recognize my own strengths and weaknesses."

True to its name, *Wild Things* is a crazy romp set against the backdrop of a privileged enclave in Miami, Florida. The story opens when devilishly handsome high school guidance counselor Sam Lombardo (Matt Dillon) is accused of rape by spoiled, golden girl Kelly Van Ryan (Denise Richards). All *seems* lost for the presumably innocent ex-heartthrob when Suzie Toller (Neve) adds another rape charge to the growing list of accusations. The plot moves as fast as its characters via many bizarre twists and over-the-top turns, leaving the viewer breathless with anticipation for the outcome of this outlandish, dark comedy.

From its inception, the movie was in danger of being misunderstood. John McNaughton, the director of *Henry: Portrait of a Serial Killer* (1990) and *Mad Dog and Glory* (1993), had no trouble recognizing the deliberately sleazy and violent film for what it was: a fun satire of human nature at its worst. "I think that probably a lot of people didn't quite see it," he explained during an interview. "The tabloid trashiness makes it fun. But if it's not handled correctly it could be trash."

The question remained, would the motion picture be able to draw the kind of talent it needed to become a success? In filmmaker McNaughton's opinion, getting a bankable star like Kevin Bacon (*JFK, A Few Good Men, Sleepers*) could make the difference between a straight-to-video or a worldwide release. However, he couldn't predict what the veteran actor's reaction would be, until, that is, he finally summoned the courage to send Bacon the script. "Kevin has a great reputation as an actor," McNaughton told the *Jerusalem Post*, "so when he came in it sort of signaled to the rest of the acting community that this wasn't a piece of trash, that it was a project of merit."

When thirty-nine-year-old Bacon initially examined the screenplay, he confused the film for a cross between TV's *Melrose Place* and cable's *Red Shoe Diaries*. "When I first picked up the script," Bacon reported to *Entertainment Weekly*, "I thought, 'Oh, my God, this is the trashiest piece of crap I've ever read.' But every few pages, I kept discovering that it wasn't what it seemed. Every few pages, there was another surprise."

Kevin was so delighted that he immediately signed on to executive produce and star in the film. Little did he know, the real surprises were just beginning. When it came time to cast the project's remaining lead roles, Robert Downey Jr. (*Chaplin, Two Girls and a Guy*) was chosen to portray the conniving guidance counselor, Sam Lombardo. However, when the film's insurance bonders labeled Downey a high-risk investment due to his well-publicized self-destructive streak, Matt Dillon (*To Die For, There's Something About Mary*) was brought in as a substitute.

The next casting hurdle involved the roles of Kelly Van Ryan and Suzie Toller. Director McNaughton had originally wanted Campbell to play Kelly, the rich homecoming queen. He was surprised to discover that Neve was more interested in appearing as the twisted jailbird, Suzie. "It's funny," he confirmed to the *Allentown* (Pennsylvania) *Morning Call*. "She wanted to play the bad girl. Neve comes from a family of tough customers. She told me members of her extended family have missing teeth. They're a real rough-and-tumble group."

Neve was determined to shake her peaches-and-cream screen image once and for all. And playing the most evil and immoral character in the movie seemed the quickest and most drastic way of accomplishing that. With a failed domestic relationship behind her and an uncertain future ahead, the actress needed to prove to herself that she could achieve anything she set her mind to—and transforming herself into a malevolent psychopath oncamera was a daunting challenge. "For me it was about playing someone very different, which ultimately is the reason I took this film," she explained to *University Wire*.

Drawn to the complexity of Suzie's personality, Neve used the onscreen character to sort through her own inner turmoil. Through her film alter ego, she could literally see how the other half lived and discover a side of herself that had yet to find a voice. She told the media, "It's so extremely opposite to anything I've done before. And it's the opposite of me in a lot of ways. It's fun, because you get to learn a lot about yourself. You have to find things within yourself that connect to the character."

As *Party of Five*'s reluctant role model, Neve had recently been honored with Family Films and Family Television's Best

Family TV Actress award. Her decision to play the lawless Suzie jarred with her G-rated reputation, and many wondered whether she was letting down her loyal TV fans. Showing a far more vocal and rebellious side than she had thus far revealed to her fans, the actress said to E! Online, "I am an actor first. I didn't choose to be a politician. I didn't ask people to follow all my steps. That's not what I'm saying. I am trying to entertain people. And I think it's a parent's responsibility to watch what their children are watching. It's not really my responsibility."

Besides splitting from husband Jeff Colt, chucking her role-model status was one of the first independent moves Neve had made in a while. She relished the idea of doing something wildly unexpected, and gleefully anticipated the effect that her bad-girl turn would have on her squeaky clean fan base. "Oh yeah," she laughed during a *Journal Arts* interview. "People will definitely be shocked seeing me this way. All of the characters in this thing are very strange. Very evil. All of them."

Wild Things also held a special place in Neve's heart because it offered her a chance to express her opinions on the individual's right to be different. The role of high school student Suzie, a bisexual teenager, gave Neve a platform from which to preach tolerance and acceptance. "The sad thing is that I find some people will feel it is more shocking. But, no, it should not be more shocking. From my point of view, I am completely OK with homosexuality, bisexuality, whatever people's sexual choices are," she expressed to *University Wire*. "And that's about love and it's about instinct and it's about your personal choices in life. And it's kind of sad that violence is more acceptable than someone's personal choice of sexuality."

Campbell could not understand why bisexuality was considered so controversial. Neve had first hand experience with the subject, and would continue to be a human rights advocate through her work. During the fifth hit season (1998–99) of *Party of Five*, Neve would exchange an onscreen kiss with actress Olivia d'Abo. In the film *Panic* (1999), starring William H. Macy and Donald Sutherland, Campbell assumes the role of a bisexual hairdresser, and in *Three to Tango* (1999) her character, Amy, recounts an affair she once had with a Brazilian girl. Neve explained to *Genre*, "Because for me it's just such a reality: You are human, I am human, let's try to accept one another for whatever we are. . . ." "Actually, one of my girlfriends came out after she and I had been friends for a couple of years. And it was really funny because she was so nervous about telling me. And when she told me I was like, 'OK, you got a beer?' It doesn't change who you are and what you mean to me."

Much like *Scream*, *Wild Things* was an outlandish satire with a keen sense of humor. Neve reveled in the quick-witted, irreverent dialogue that was characteristic of the script. "But it was also about the fact of understanding the humor within it," Neve confirmed to *University Wire*. "And understanding that the world can be absurd in many ways and playing on that."

Although she had shown an active interest in portraying Suzie Toller, getting signed on for the screen role was by no means an easy proposition. The director was not yet sold on the idea of her playing the bad girl. The opposition Neve encountered was a result of the no-nudity clause that was a condition of her participation. Her decision to keep herself under wraps, however, had very little to do with modesty and everything to do with artistic necessity. "It's a personal choice. I have nothing against anybody who makes the opposite choice," she clarified for TNT cable TV's *Rough Cut* Web site. "If it had something to do with the character—I did full back nudity once for a [Canadian] movie called *Baree* [1994]. But my character was half-Native American and half-white, and she was skinny-dipping in a lake out in the wilderness with a wolf, and it was necessary to establish that the character was very free. I didn't feel that it was necessary for this character. I didn't feel it was going to enhance the character in any way to do nudity. Also, I don't feel comfortable with nudity that is just for graphic sex or box-office draw."

McNaughton was reluctant to bow to Campbell's contractual stipulations. He believed that Suzie Toller's character dictated showing her body oncamera. The shrewd director tried to push the issue as long as he could, but finally acquiesced upon realizing that his potential leading lady was not budging from her position. "Well, Neve was riding very high and the studio [Columbia Tri-Star] was very interested in her for the role. So she came in and, personally, I liked her very much," he told *University Wire*. "I saw *Scream* and I really thought she had believability. But the nudity was an issue, so we discussed it and decided, in a very friendly way, 'Maybe some other time.' It just didn't seem it would work out. She has a television career and she has to be careful and, whatever her personal feelings are, it's her life and her body and it's fine with me. She was so personally nice and genuine and unpretentious, and I liked her very much. But it didn't seem it was going to work. Then we saw a number of other actors and Neve started to look better and better so she came back and we said, 'Here's what we can do, here's what we can't do.'"

In the end, Campbell got the terms she sought. The film was altered to reflect her personal boundaries and limitations. "You see my bare back in this film. You wouldn't believe the stuff that goes into my contract," she explained to *Journal Arts*. "'No side of breast, no nipple, only down to the small of the back,' and so on. You need to set those boundaries before you get on the set."

Neve's conviction and determination to protect herself from exploitation was admirable. Only a few young actresses in Hollywood today could take such full charge of a professional situation and succeed. "I want to control my own career," Neve specified to the *Buffalo News*. "That's how I was brought up: to fight for the control of my own destiny. I come from a family of fighters."

Having ironed out the details of the movie contract, Neve found herself wondering anew if she had made the right choice. Was the film worth possibly throwing away her professional reputation and status as a role model? Up till then she had made savvy decisions about her career. That didn't stop her, however, from worrying every step of the way. "There's definitely apprehensions when you choose to do a film and to do a role that is very different from anything you've ever done," she reported to *Entertainment Tonight*. "On the other hand, I wanted to be courageous about that—you know my plan, hopefully, is that I have some longevity in my career and that I play all different kinds of characters. And I keep challenging myself, so for me the fun and the challenge outweigh the apprehension."

As she continued to ponder the wisdom of her decision, an unexpected encounter gave her some much-needed perspective. "I met Robert De Niro last year at the Martin Scorsese tribute, and I was lucky enough to sit at his table," she described the experience to E! Online. "I was really intimidated. I never get intimidated, but I was, like, what do you say to Robert De Niro? But I was going to do *Wild Things* with John McNaughton, and De Niro had worked with him on *Mad Dog and Glory* [1993]. I told him I was worried about this role, because it was very extreme and very different from what I'd done. He said, 'You know what? You're young. Do the movie. If it's a mistake, you're still young.' And that was pretty great."

De Niro's sage advice could not have come at a better time. With renewed determination, Campbell set about effecting a transformation that was guaranteed to startle her fans. To research the role of Suzie, Neve visited a Florida correctional facility and spoke with female prisoners. "I met a young woman [inmate] and we were supposed to talk about half an hour but we ended up talking for about four hours because we really hit it off," she relayed to

Entertainment Weekly. "She expressed to me why she made certain decisions in her life and why her life had gone in such a bad way and what the experience was to be in jail."

Neve's devotion to her craft was further evidenced by the physical alterations she made for the sake of the new project. To give herself a more edgy and tough look, she restyled her hair and applied temporary tattoos. The metamorphosis from girl-next-door to girl-next-trailer was so drastic, she even scared herself. "The look was especially important, because my audience really needs to not see Julia [Salinger of *Party of Five*] in this perform-ance," she reported to *Journal Arts.* "I wanted to veer away from that. So we punked up my hair, got tattoos, short shorts. The first time they did all that in makeup, I scared myself. I wouldn't want to meet that girl in a dark alley."

Taking the transformation even further, Neve decided to mimic the bulging-biceps look made famous by actress Linda Hamilton in *Terminator 2: Judgment Day* (1991). She began lifting weights and training in her free time. "Suzie was a drug addict and spent a lot of time in prison," she told *USA Today.* "All they do in prison is work out."

Neve took her new image and attitude to the streets of Miami, where the movie was to be filmed. She wanted to feel what it would be like to be Suzie in an everyday context—how people would react to her, and whether or not they would recognize the person underneath the getup. The discoveries she made on her outing to a convenience store were not only eye-opening, but downright appalling. She recounted to the *Allentown* (Pennsylva-nia) *Morning Call:* "I'll never forget. I walked in and no one rec-ognized me. None of the people behind the counter would serve me because of the way that I looked. Then they followed me around to see if I would shoplift anything. It was really interesting; it helped me understand why punks go to even further extremes,

NEVE CAMPBELL

because it made me want to do more, to be even more shocking. Then the storeowners started apologizing, which made me even angrier. What difference does it make who I am? They should be serving everyone with the same courtesy."

Her field research completed, Neve was all set to begin work in Miami. While some stars are happy just to get a nice trailer on a film location, she was offered a spacious yellow house for the duration of the shoot, complete with graceful chandeliers, an ornate staircase, and large potted plants. The manor even boasted a pond filled with live koi. Campbell was visibly impressed upon seeing her home away from home for the first time.

Living it up in the lap of luxury during the summer of 1997, was only one of the many pleasant surprises awaiting Neve on *Wild Things*. Getting the chance to work with the notable cast and director was like a dream come true. "John McNaughton, the director, is known for . . . films that are very extreme," she told *Entertainment Tonight*. "So he's a very interesting man to work with. Matt Dillon, Kevin Bacon, Bill Murray, you can't beat that. They're wonderful and talented and inspiring and really down to earth and a lot of fun. And it was really great working with new people as well like Daphne [Rubin-Vega] and Denise [Richards]! It was good."

As two of the youngest ensemble players, Neve and Denise Richards spent time getting to know each other on and off the set. Acting alongside Campbell was an experience Denise would not soon forget. "I really like Neve. She's very down to earth. She's a really nice girl, and we just got along," Richards told *University Wire*. "And I think they also wanted to see the chemistry between the two girls. When I auditioned, she was there to see how we worked together and if there was chemistry there and how we looked next to each other. But I liked working with her; we've become friends."

The group of actors may have gotten along splendidly, but all the camaraderie in the world couldn't help them make heads or tails out of the screenplay's deliberately convoluted plot twists. To determine their motivation in each scene, the cast had to gather with the director, writers, and producers to establish the sequence of events. "We'd sit in rehearsals trying to piece together what was going on in the script, who we were lying to about what, and it'd just get so complicated we'd have to stop and rest," Kevin Bacon later told *Entertainment Weekly*.

As if to add to the already overwhelming confusion on the set, a tornado came within a mile of their base camp in Miami, halting production for a full day. With that calamity safely behind them, another problem surfaced at the most inopportune time. "It was odd," Neve recalled during an *Entertainment Tonight* interview. "Kevin Bacon, Daphne Rubin-Vega, and I were shooting a scene together next to a swamp and all of the sudden one of the crew says 'Cut!'—it was one of the lighting guys—and they said there was a dead body in the water. And so the cops came by and were like 'You makin' a movie?' And we were like 'Yeah.' So they actually—typical Hollywood—held the body next to the dock so it wouldn't float through the shot so we could finish the scene."

While the tornado and floating corpse incident made for great media copy, reporters covering the film were far more intrigued by the notorious oncamera make-out session between Neve and Denise Richards. While the script's same-sex encounter was a first for Campbell, she wasn't any more worried about kissing a woman onscreen than she would be kissing a man oncamera. In her opinion, both situations would be equally discomforting in such a public forum. "Honestly, doing any kind of love scene is an awkward experience. I mean, how many jobs are there out there where you're asked to take off your clothes with people who are strangers—an audience or crew—and make out," she revealed to TNT's *Rough Cut* Web site.

After calming herself with a few drinks, Neve tried to soothe Denise's frazzled nerves. "I think it was a touchy scene to do because Denise wasn't extremely comfortable with the nudity. So it was about making her comfortable and talking about her perimeters and all her other boundaries, deciding what we were comfortable with and what we weren't comfortable with and being professional about it. And we had a bottle of wine. In fact, we had margaritas, some tequila and some wine."

To the actresses' chagrin, their preparations for the scene were for naught. The director had to make a hasty exit that day due to illness. The highly anticipated sequence was rescheduled for several weeks later.

Neve and Denise had to prepare all over again for the intimate onscreen encounter. The second time around they set aside a few hours before the shoot to address the difficulties they were having with the scene. "My feeling on sex scenes is that once you commit to doing it, you can't feel uncomfortable about it," Neve told the *Buffalo News*. "Audiences will sense that you're uncomfortable, and you can't allow that. So you have to find ways to be comfortable, and that's the reason I drank. Before we started drinking, though, we sat down and discussed the scene."

While Campbell may have considered doing a love scene in front of a roomful of strangers difficult, she was even more uncomfortable revealing her onscreen exploits to her real-life mother. When the time came to premiere *Wild Things* on March 6, 1998, at the GCC Hollywood Galaxy Theatre in Los Angeles, Neve encouraged her mom, Marnie, and her brother, Christian, to attend the star-studded event. Everything was going smoothly until she saw herself cavorting in a *ménage à trois* onscreen with Richards and Dillon. Christian reported to *Time International* on the screening, "I could see her [Neve] sink into her seat during the make-out scenes."

Campbell never got the chance to sink too low in her cinema seat. While she was naturally embarrassed by the footage, Marnie gave her daughter moral support. Her understanding did a lot to alleviate her daughter's discomfort. "Mom is an artist," Neve told the *Jerusalem Post*. "She totally understands the process. As I was sinking into the chair for some of the scenes, she'd take my hand and say, 'It's OK, honey.' She was great."

The *Wild Things* debut was met with mixed reviews. Some of the audience had difficulty with the film's overt sexuality and violence. Not recognizing it as a spoof, many viewers considered the picture to be in bad taste. "It's fun for me now to sit back and watch an audience which really doesn't know what to expect," Kevin Bacon commented to the *Jerusalem Post*. "There's two sides to that. In a way, it's kind of neat, because people are not quite sure what they're supposed to be thinking and feeling. They kind of go 'Am I allowed to laugh at this at all? Or is this just like so bad? Are they serious?' The other side of it is that it creates certain inherent problems in marketing the picture. I mean, I almost want to put a disclaimer on the poster that says 'We don't take this too seriously, so we hope that you don't either,' you know?"

Whereas some filmgoers may not have gotten the plot jokes, reviewers praised the new release for the deftness with which it managed its slippery subject matter. They also noticed Neve's new dimension onscreen. A critic for *People* expressed, "Dillon is impressive, Richards is wall-poster hot, Bacon is stonily effective as the investigating cop, and Campbell, as a stoner outcast, has fun flexing more acting muscles here than she used in her *Scream* outings." Giving *Wild Things* a solid B rating, *Entertainment Weekly* also praised Neve's breakthrough performance, writing, "In *Wild Things*, a tricky-bordering-on-gimmicky film noir with a glaze of soft-core kink, Neve Campbell, who glided through *The Craft* and the two *Screams* with such unfussy finesse that she threatened to disappear on screen, makes a far punchier impact in what might be described as the Fairuza Balk role." Made on a budget of

$20 million, *Wild Things* grossed a disappointing $29.7 million in its fourteen-week U.S. theatrical run.

Despite the modest response to *Wild Things,* Neve was generally pleased with the finished film. The movie was not about ending world hunger or making a lasting artistic impression. For Campbell, *Wild Things* was simply about cutting loose and showing the world that there was more to her than met the eye. The critics' reaction showed that she had, once again, made good on her creative promise to herself.

Ten

GOING THROUGH THE MOTIONS

s if completing *Wild Things* in the summer of 1997 wasn't enough, Neve revved up her vocal chords once more to begin work on the highly anticipated big-screen sequel to *Scream*. Just two days after she wrapped production for *Wild Things*, she was off to Atlanta, Georgia, to reunite with the surviving cast of characters from the original feature.

Although Campbell had already agreed to appear in the follow-up, she was not convinced that it could meet the expectations established by the original. "I did have reservations about doing a sequel to *Scream* despite the fact I was already contracted to do it," she admitted to the *Ottawa Citizen*. "I had apprehensions because the only reason any sequel is ever made is that the first one was so good. You think—who are we to try and outdo ourselves? But I was incredibly happy when I got Kevin's [Williamson] script. I thought it was . . . funnier and scarier."

Fans were anxious to see what their beloved horror heroine's return to the big screen would produce. Neve, however, wanted to avoid merely duplicating her first performance as everybody's favorite victim, Sidney Prescott. She worried about getting bored with the part, and, in turn, disappointing her viewing audience. Instead she decided to reflect the passage of time by bringing something new to the film role. As she explained to the media, "I definitely decided I didn't want to be playing the same character again, so it's important that the new film takes place two years later. This is someone who's been through an incredible amount of trauma in her life and has needed to get away from her home town and develop new relationships."

Because *Scream* had been such an instant hit with moviegoers in 1996, plans to release the sequel less than a year after the debut of the original came as a pleasant surprise to its many devotees. When Miramax Films announced an early December 1997 release critics argued that the studio was trying to exploit a formula and would not be able to deliver the goods come showtime. According to Miramax's Bob Weinstein, however, a sequel had been in the works for some time. "This is not the classic case of going 'Wow, we made a lotta money, can we make another one quick?'" he communicated to *Entertainment Weekly*. "We always saw this as a trilogy of movies. It's like George Lucas's plan for *Star Wars*, only here we're dealing with a knife-wielding killer in a mask."

Weinstein was also betting on moviegoers' attachment to the surviving characters. The clever studio exec decided to simply give the fans what they wanted and let nature take its course. "Based on the reaction to the first movie, we realized this was more than a sequel," Weinstein explained to the *Los Angeles Times*. "It's playing more like a continuous serial because it's the same characters that survived the first movie and people have an affinity for these characters."

Though everyone involved with the film, including director Wes Craven, had to work overtime to meet the planned December 12, 1997, release date, scriptwriter Kevin Williamson was hardest hit when it came to delivering his drop-dead-funny dialogue on time. "As soon as the [original] film reached $50 million, everyone at Miramax was chanting 'Sequel,'" Williamson told *Entertainment Weekly*. "I cranked it out in about three weeks, turning in ten pages at a time."

The young screenwriter was busy working on his new TV series, *Dawson's Creek* (1998–present), when news of the sequel finally broke. "I can't handle it—I'm slowly self-destructing," he panicked in a recollection for a *Newsday* interview on January 18, 1998. "Soon I'll be totally burned out, another hot new writer will come along to take my place and I'll be back at the bottom."

Writing two very different projects simultaneously, Williamson soon found himself under surveillance in North Carolina where *Dawson's Creek* was shooting. As he told *Entertainment Weekly*. "They [Miramax executives] came to harass me, and to make sure I wasn't going to eat, sleep, or breathe anything other than the plot of *Scream 2*."

Many sleepless nights later, Williamson finally came up with the premise that would drive the success of *Scream 2*. Two years have passed, and Sidney is safely tucked away at Windsor College. Meanwhile, Gale Weathers (Courteney Cox) has written a true-crime memoir about the Woodsboro murders featured in the first *Scream*. When her book is made into a movie titled *Stab*, a copy-cat killer offs two innocent students, played by Jada Pinkett and Omar Epps, at the premiere. Sidney tries to ignore the resurgence of her past. However, when the murderer strikes at her college, killing a rule-abiding sorority sister in the process, she is forced to fight back.

Returning cast members included Neve Campbell (Sidney Prescott), Courteney Cox (Gale Weathers), David Arquette (Deputy Dewey Riley), Liev Schreiber (Cotton Weary), and Jamie Kennedy (Randy Meeks). Nearly every available young actor in Hollywood was clamoring to audition for the sequel. "After the success of the first one," Craven told *Entertainment Weekly*, "we could get any young actor we wanted. They were breaking down doors to get into the sequel. The idea that [the star of TV's] *Buffy the Vampire Slayer* has a relatively minor role shows you how big this thing is."

Sarah Michelle Gellar (*Buffy the Vampire Slayer, I Know What You Did Last Summer*) confirmed Craven's report, saying, "I so desperately wanted to be a part of this movie. I called my agent and I was like, 'Please, please, please, please get me in this movie.' It just had a cool feeling about it."

Besides twenty-year-old Gellar, the new members on board included Duane Martin (*Above the Rim*), Heather Graham (*Boogie Nights, Lost in Space*), Laurie Metcalf (TV's *Roseanne*), Tori Spelling (TV's *Beverly Hills, 90210*), Rebecca Gayheart (TV's *Beverly Hills, 90210, Loving*), Jada Pinkett (*The Nutty Professor*), and Jerry O'Connell (*Jerry Maguire*, TV's sci-fi adventure series *Sliders*).

The secrecy surrounding *Scream 2* created some casting roadblocks. Fearing that the plot sequences might be revealed to the public before *Scream 2*'s release, the producers couldn't risk sending the script around town. So they printed it on dark brown paper with red lines running through the dialogue (to make it difficult for the script to be duplicated), and hand-delivered each copy to its rightful owner. "We were trying to cast without a screenplay, with very vague characterizations," producer Cathy Konrad told the *Los Angeles Times*. "Scripts, minus a lot of pages, were taken to people's houses. I felt like an idiot. I told agents not to read the script, but that didn't fly. I felt kind of awkward. I told people, 'I know this is really silly, but this is what we gotta do.' To a certain extent, it let people know we cared about keeping the thrill out there for audiences. The fun on the first one was because it was so unexpected. We wanted to try not to let everybody know what happened in this one."

The plot thickened when forty pages of Kevin Williamson's first draft of *Scream 2* were posted on the Internet, only days after he turned it into the studio. After rewriting the segment, Williamson and the production team decided to keep the original copy literally under lock and key. "When I first got the script," actor Jerry O'Connell joked with *Entertainment Weekly*, "two men with Uzis delivered it and stayed with me until I was done reading it."

The cast was sworn to secrecy, but that wasn't enough peace of mind for Miramax. The movie was shot out of sequence so even its stars wouldn't know how the story panned out. Several cast members would show up at the premiere just to see how the thriller ended. "It was weird, it was the first time I had to do this," Wes Craven told the *Los Angeles Times*. "It was a murder mystery, so we had to protect the identity of the culprit or culprits. We just got very security-minded. . . . People had to wear badges to get on the set. Our weakness was the group scenes—there were several set at movie theaters. The opening scene is set in a movie theater, and was described very accurately on the Internet."

Originally scheduled as an eight-week shoot, *Scream 2* was limited to a frenzied four-week production schedule to meet the early December release date. Wes Craven chose Atlanta for the film's location so he could use the scenic Agnes Scott College as a backdrop, describing it to the *Atlanta Journal and Constitution* as a "unique combination of a small, human-scaled campus, interesting architecture both interior and exterior."

The stress of making *Scream 2* was soon taking a collective toll on everyone involved. With so little time before the release, the cast and crew had to work overtime to complete the project. The extremely humid conditions didn't help matters any, nor did the accidental destruction of a full day's reel of film while en route to Los Angeles.

Kevin Williamson was also having trouble finishing the script. He carried the last fifteen pages around in his head for weeks before finally putting the words down on paper. In the end, Williamson was convinced that all the hard work, secrecy, and planning had paid off. "We're hip to the fact that we're a sequel," he warned the *Atlanta Journal and Constitution*. "In the first film, we sent up all the horror movies that came before it. In this one, we send up *Scream* to a large degree."

On December 10, 1997, *Scream 2* premiered at Mann's Chinese Theatre in Hollywood. The stars in attendance had only good things to say about the long-awaited sequel. Opening on 3,112 screens nationwide, *Scream 2* pulled in a record-breaking $39.2 million at the box office during its first week, making it the all-time highest-grossing film to date for the month of December. With a $24 million production budget, a $28 million marketing campaign, and a $106.8 million domestic gross, the release of *Scream 2* cemented Hollywood's hold on the horror genre. The sequel (in the tradition of *Aliens 2* and *The Godfather Part II*) had lived up to, and even surpassed, the original. A critic from TNT's *Rough Cut* Web site confirmed, "Like the original, *Scream 2* keeps you guessing the killer's identity right up until the very end. But this isn't just a copycat movie. Scarier and funnier than the original, *Scream 2* takes the horror movie send-up in a proper, new direction—spoofing the horror movie sequel." A reviewer for the CNN network enthused, "While having seen the original will enhance your enjoyment of this sequel, it works well as a satirical stand-alone. *Scream 2* is a lethally entertaining piece of moviemaking that will have audiences shrieking . . . with laughter."

Because her groundbreaking reprisal of Sidney Prescott stood out from the rest of the performances in *Scream 2*, Neve earned the Blockbuster and MTV Movie Awards for best actress (upsetting

Titanic's Kate Winslet, among other favorites). It seemed that the Midas touch Campbell had displayed throughout her career once again was working its magic. Winning the MTV Movie Award, the Oscar of the new generation, was especially sweet because it came from her peers. But instead of reveling in the spotlight while giving her acceptance speech, the young actress looked somewhat frazzled and tired in her floor-length black gown and new cropped hairstyle. "Thank you very much…I had a blast doing *Scream 2*, I had a really good time and as an actor when you take on a horror film, whether it be a fantastic script or not, you never really think you're gonna get an award. So this is . . . this is really cool and I'm just glad to see that the audiences loved it, and MTV viewers loved it, and so thank you to my team and to the cast, and to the people I worked with and to the audience."

Toward the end of filming *Scream 2*, Neve was trying to, once again, reconcile her six-year long contractual obligation to *Party of Five* and the demands of her thriving movie career. While the popular TV series, which was already in its fourth season (1997–98), was showing no signs of malaise, the same could not be said of Campbell. "It's definitely a challenge as an actor, to be playing a character in a fourth year," she told the *Los Angeles Times*. "The writing is still fantastic, but as an actor, [I don't feel] it's new anymore, so it doesn't feel as inspiring. The premise that they started with does have to go out the window at a certain point. That doesn't mean the characters aren't still interesting in some way, and that people aren't interested in what happens to them."

Heading back to her familiar *Party of Five* set on the Sony Pictures lot in Culver City, Neve was relieved that everything was just as she'd left it. The cast was still unaffected, the writing was still on course, and the mood was still optimistic. Moreover, the ratings were going through the roof. "We're getting like a million more people watching every week. It's been remarkable, you know," executive Chris Keyser told CNN. "Shows hope for things like this."

In its new season, the very successful *Party of Five* would still have many challenges to overcome. One of which was the growing demands made on its cast members. Besides Neve's star turn in films, Lacey Chabert was receiving many offers after appearing in *Lost in Space* (1998). Meanwhile, Jennifer Love Hewitt had also been keeping busy, starring in Kevin Williamson's horror films *I Know What You Did Last Summer* (1997) and *I Still Know What You Did Last Summer* (1998), as well as the teen joyride, *Can't Hardly Wait* (1998).

While the women of *Party of Five* had been busy making headlines, the show's male stars—Scott Wolf and Matthew Fox— kept a lower profile on hiatus. Despite his appearances in *White Squall* (1996) and *The Evening Star* (1997), Wolf preferred to use most of his downtime for rest and relaxation. As a new daddy, Fox's priority during season breaks had been to be with his new family. "Oh God, I want to be there and be present every second that I possibly can," he confirmed to *People*. "Being a father is something I'm looking forward to with incredible anticipation."

With Neve, Lacey Chabert, and Jennifer Love Hewitt all trying to expand their professional horizons, *Party of Five*'s production team had to make adjustments and accommodations. Realizing that the stars' success in features would reflect positively on the series, co-creators and co-producers Chris Keyser and Amy Lippman made every effort to reconcile the scheduling conflicts.

The support Neve received from her *Party of Five* family was considerable. There were no hard feelings and no rivalry. Much like a real-life family, the success of one member was considered to be a collective victory. Amy Lippman was one of Campbell's biggest champions throughout her transition into big-screen films. Having seen how far Neve had come since her early days on *Party of Five* in 1994, she couldn't help but be impressed with the actress's wise career choices. In the *Los Angeles Times*, she reflected upon Campbell's decision to star in *Scream*, saying, "It's funny—I wouldn't have suggested that career move, but Neve has made some interesting choices. She's been shrewd—if you look at it on the page, the move from a quality drama to a horror film doesn't seem to be a move you'd want to make, but she carefully considered it, and it obviously was a great move for her. It won her a lot of notoriety, and a lot of other opportunities."

The rest of the cast was equally encouraging of Neve's ever-growing popularity. Neve and Jennifer Love Hewitt, six years her junior, had plenty of chances to compare their screams, as well as give each other tips on their burgeoning film careers, on the *Party* set. Although grossing only half as much as the *Scream* films, Hewitt's first two horror movies, *I Know What You Did Last Summer* and *I Still Know What You Did Last Summer*, established a common ground between the two women. Sixteen-year-old Lacey Chabert, who was just coming off a costarring role in *Lost in Space* (which grossed $69 million), also had a positive reaction to Neve's achievements. "She always goes for the complex, unpredictable thing, and I admire her for it," she explained to *TV Guide*.

As Campbell was often tired on the Sony Pictures set, she found herself retreating more and more to the quiet of her trailer for rest and relaxation. Increasingly, the production crew noticed her fragile state, and tried to help her in any way possible. Scott Wolf reflected on Neve's state of mind during the start of season four, "I don't think you can do everything she's doing and not be tired and frustrated sometimes. But she's still Neve like I know her. She's still always laughing and smiling."

Trying to perk up her flagging spirits at a time when she would rather have escaped from her TV responsibilities, Neve put up a good front for her *Party of Five* family. Because she valued the reassurance of her old friends, she never dreamt of leaving them prior to her contract's expiration.

If her TV castmates hadn't meant so much to her, Neve might have bolted the hit series. The camaraderie, however, was a double-edged sword; spending too much time with the Salinger family was also beginning to take its toll. No matter how hard she tried, she couldn't deny her desire for new experiences and new associations. "Whenever there's a birthday or a concert or something, we'll all go out," she revealed to *Sassy*. "But it's a little harder for us to go out together now because people recognize us, and it's a bummer to get interrupted in the middle of a nice meal, you know? But we're really not doing the weekly thing anymore. We're together twelve and thirteen hours a day, and you can only spend so much time with people. No offense to my costars, but some days it's like, 'Get me out of here!' "

Just as she had outgrown her relationship with Jeff Colt, Neve was beginning to do the same with *Party of Five*. It was only natural that she would move beyond the series. At some point Neve's appearance was bound to reflect her mature frame of mind. "Julia will be 20 when I'm 26. [Julia's] been in high school for a long time—and I didn't even graduate high school. I didn't like it then! I want to play my age, and I've started doing that in my other roles now. No matter how good you are as an actor, you grow up. Your face grows up. I have a sophistication about me now."

Campbell's other complaint about *Party of Five* was the repetitive plot lines that are characteristic of many long-running TV shows. Part of what had attracted her to the series was the originality of its writing. Gradually, she began to doubt the writers' ability to generate further new and interesting story ideas. "Like any job, you do it long enough, and it becomes tedious," she explained to *Time International*. "And although I love my show, it is somewhat tedious playing my character. There are only so many plot lines in the world, and we've done them all."

Neve's doubts were by no means off the mark. Chris Keyser and Amy Lippman had been grappling with keeping the Fox TV offering fresh and exciting for the past two seasons. Exploring topics like Julia's troubled marriage to Griffin (Jeremy London), Griffin and Bailey each being unfaithful to their mates, Claudia's teenage rebellion, and Charlie's hospitalization for cancer, the producers and writers tried to infuse the dramatic TV series with new life. "By the beginning of the third season [1996–97], we decided we wanted to turn things around a bit," Keyser confirmed to *People* online. "Amy wanted to readjust the show periodically. It becomes harder and harder not to repeat yourself and to come up with plots that are believable."

No matter what happened, the success of an hour-long weekly show required all of its stars to continue working on the property. The producers were dead-set against replacing any of the regulars, and worked hard to make sure that everyone, including Neve, was happy with the show's ongoing development. "It works both ways—we don't get their name on contract, then cackle, 'They're mine for six years!' We have an obligation to constantly examine the characters and keep their personalities in flux," Lippman conveyed to the *Los Angeles Times*. "Every year, at the end of the season, we ask ourselves, 'Where did we leave the characters, and how can we change? This series is about a family. You can't tell the story with half the family there; we have never written a principle character out of an episode, and never will."

Realizing that the program's popularity depended on the group's collective effort, Campbell refused to be the one responsible for breaking up the *Party*. Every cast member had an immense loyalty to the show. They were all there at the start of *Party of Five* and they would all be there for its final oncamera moments. "Well, you don't want to let down the people who have helped you out," Neve told *Rolling Stone*. "And, also, what's it gonna be, *Party of Four*? It's one of those circumstances where it's not really possible, because the show is about us."

Despite her loyalty, by the 1997–98 season, it was clear that Neve was not thrilled with having to work on *Party of Five* for the duration of her contract. Of course, counterbalancing that were many positive aspects to working with the *Party of Five* crew, producers, and costars. By now, Neve was confident that a career in film would be waiting for her by the time her contractual obligation was fulfilled in April 2000. She decided that if nothing else, *Party of Five* would save her from the dreaded fate of overexposure. "As crazy as things might seem now, it could be going a lot faster," she told the *Buffalo News*. "People keep asking me if I wish I didn't have a TV series because then I would be able to be in more movies, but I think *Party of Five* is a good thing in that way. It's holding me back from doing too much. Having too many movies out at once can be a bad thing," she added. "If this is the pace my career is meant to go at, I don't want to question that. If it speeds up or slows down at some point, that's what was meant to be."

For all her frustrations, disappointments, and restlessness, *Party of Five* was, in many ways, Neve's saving grace professionally. It was right around the time when *Party of Five* was beginning to gain momentum in 1996 that the idea of television stars moving into feature films had become more viable. The absence, therefore, of other quality teenage shows gave Neve the opportunity to make her transition. "I don't know what the explanation is except that we're being allowed the opportunity to be out there doing good work," Neve explained to the *Los Angeles Times*. "If I was on *Beverly Hills, 90210*, people wouldn't see me in the light they see me in. We have good dialogue, and it's being appreciated—it wasn't just a teen smash, and it took a while. It was the little train that could. The critics have been good to us, the Golden Globe award, I think we got noticed in that way, that it was about quality not quantity, and that's why we've been able to move on to other things and be trusted that we'll do good work."

Jennifer Love Hewitt also credits her success in movies to *Party of Five*, telling the *Hollywood Reporter*, "Working in films is something fun for me to do to keep myself busy, but I'm the first to say that the reason I get to do them is because of *Party of Five*. It's truly the best job I've ever had."

While *Party of Five*'s quality writing and talented cast may have had a lot to do with the cast members' crossover potential, the age of its stars was also a draw for the studios. "Really, it's a demographic situation," producer Cathy Konrad explained in the *Los Angeles Times*. "*Friends* is skewed just three years older than the movement in the world right now. People love the characters, but as the timeline of cycles hit, the *Party of Five* cast has a lot of characters and faces that speak to a much bigger demographic. Those kids are not 'Reality Bites' kids, they're perceived as more accessible than grunge Gen-Xers."

The box-office triumphs of *Scream* and *Scream 2* went a long way in shifting the entertainment industry's focus, paving the way for a resurgence in teen-oriented movies and television shows. "Studios are just starting to recognize this market and what it can do," Robert Bucksbaum, an entertainment analyst with Reel Source Inc., told *USA Today*. "This market has been neglected for many years. But if you go to any mall, which is where all the movie complexes are going these days, they're just crowded with kids."

It wasn't only the film industry that was tapping into the teenage vibe. Pop music—driven by the selling power of such hot groups as Hanson, Backstreet Boys, and the Spice Girls—was also cornering the youth market. Television producers were anxious to exploit this trend, and teen-oriented music groups could be found working steadily on such shows as *Dawson's Creek*, *Buffy the Vampire Slayer*, *Felicity*, and *That '70s Show*. The reason for all this? Simply put, favorable demographics.

The Census Bureau reported that there are 37 million ten-to-nineteen-year-olds in the United States today. That number is expected to increase, with an estimated 42 million by the next decade. Teenagers also have more spending power than ever before, boasting an estimated $82 billion in disposable income annually. While all the studios had to do was check the latest demographic figures, it took the box-office results of both *Screams* to hammer that point home to the film industry.

The last to jump on the teenage bandwagon, movie studios are suddenly running around searching for the next new sensation. "The teenage population is growing faster than any other segment," Paramount executive Rob Friedman said in a *USA Today* interview, "and their tastes are more sophisticated than they used to be."

The years 1997 and 1998 were rife with movies and television shows geared toward younger people. Studios were notorious for turning down quality projects just because they were unsuited to the newly reigning demographic. "Everything is being cast younger in Hollywood," Cathy Konrad told *Time*. "You'll read a script where the characters are forty years old, and the studio will ask if they can be in their early twenties instead."

In the 1980s, director John Hughes had been the most accomplished chronicler of teen angst, penning such screen hits as *Sixteen Candles*, *Pretty in Pink*, and *The Breakfast Club*. Until the 1990s teen explosion, young people were forced to fall back on these cult classics they could "relate to" for much-needed entertainment. Late 1990s films like *Disturbing Behavior*, *Can't Hardly Wait*, *She's All That*, *Varsity Blues*, *Cruel Intentions*, and *Teaching Mrs. Tingle* have toppled the John Hughes dynasty. Of course, there is a significant difference between these recent entries and the teenage movies of the 1980s. Earlier films never boasted casts so filled with popular television stars.

Because television shows like WB's *Buffy the Vampire Slayer*, *Dawson's Creek*, and *Felicity*, and Fox's *Party of Five* were drawing the prized 18–49-year-old demographic, studios began giving these TV favorites close scrutiny. Tube-generated teen icons like Sarah Michelle Gellar, Katie Holmes, James Van Der Beek, Jennifer Love Hewitt, and, of course, Neve Campbell were soon on every movie casting director's wish list.

Producer David Gerber commented on the changing face of casting procedures, telling the *New York Daily News*, "It used to be that we would turn to series stars to be in TV movies. Now it's almost impossible to get any of the young performers. The motion picture studios are lined up to hire them."

The ready-made fan base of television stars was a major consideration for studio executives. Luring even half of *Party of Five*'s fans into theatres would give a huge boost to ticket sales. That factor alone, however, wasn't responsible for keeping the teen beat on track. While most established leading feature film actors demand anywhere from $5 to $20 million per project, the relatively "cheap" labor provided by the tube pack was an added bonus. Young up-and-comers routinely settle for pay days well below the one million dollar mark.

The reasoning may have been sound, but the profit margin of late 1990s big screen teen flicks wasn't always up to snuff. Besides the success of *Scream*, *Scream 2*, *I Know What You Did Last Summer* ($72 million), *Varsity Blues* ($53 million), and *She's All That* ($59 million), few youth-targeted movies lived up to the studios' expectations. For example, *Disturbing Behavior* (Katie Holmes) scared up a sparse $17 million gross against a $15 million production budget, *Can't Hardly Wait* (Jennifer Love Hewitt) earned

$25 million, and *Jawbreaker* (Rose McGowan, Rebecca Gayheart) choked on $3 million. These figures proved that underestimating the intelligence of the teenage audience wasn't the foolproof get-rich-quick scheme it was in the time of the *Porky's* trilogy in the 1980s. Even putting a household name into a film was not enough to score big at the box office. The savvy generation Y refused to be exploited, shunning those movies that traded substance for style and top-40 soundtracks.

As one of the founding members of the current booming teen market, twenty-six-year-old Neve Campbell was in a position to call the shots in Hollywood. While some female celebrities were blatantly using their television authority to get themselves on the big screen, Neve was craftily carving out a new niche for herself. Once she recognized the teensploitation trend in Hollywood, Neve flatly refused to participate in any upcoming flicks set in high school or college. She was determined to avoid being grouped with the myriad of actors trying to capitalize on the latest trends.

As far as Neve's professional priorities were concerned, they were as focused as ever. But when it came to organizing her personal life, she was once again selling herself short. Ranked third in *Empire* magazine's 100 sexiest movie stars of 1998, and named one of *People* magazine's 50 Most Beautiful People of the same year, Campbell's beauty and allure were undeniable. But ironically, while her professional popularity was soaring, her love life was suffering as a result of chronic workaholism. In the wake of her divorce from Jeff in 1997, she shied away from serious relationships. Preferring to let her emotional wounds heal before entering another liaison, Neve rejected all potential suitors.

Then, too, her consuming schedule made it difficult to date. She was constantly being shuttled back and forth from one project to another, and she was sure no one outside of the business would understand the demands made on her. Fame was also standing in the way of her personal life. As *the* Neve Campbell, she had to be careful when meeting new people. She was worried that non-actors would either be intimidated by her popularity or would want to date her solely because of it. Of course, neither scenario was acceptable. "I mean, in the end, with anyone you meet, you have to be aware of the fact that it is possible that they could be with you for the wrong reasons," she told *Detour*.

The irony of Neve's predicament was that while she craved normalcy, preferring the company of individuals who weren't involved in the entertainment industry, her dating options seemed limited to actors. "It's an odd thing," she told *UniverCity*. "Actors have the same schedule so they're more understanding. How many people who work nine to five would understand why I work fourteen- to sixteen-hour days and travel every other weekend, or travel four to five months at a time. But another actor will understand that . . . so, it's a Catch 22."

Reconciling herself to that fact, Neve began a brief but memorable romance with her twenty-seven-year-old *Scream* costar, Matthew Lillard. He later described it as "one of the best relationships" he'd ever had. Although the union only lasted a short while, Campbell emerged having learned an important lesson: "I try desperately hard not to be suspicious of people," she confided in *Mademoiselle*. "It's difficult enough getting to know someone under normal circumstances. But if I spend the rest of my life being guarded, I'm not going to experience much, am I?"

Neve was also learning valuable lessons about social intimacy. Whereas her Scottish-immigrant family had taught her to be self-contained and not to burden anyone with her troubles, she was now becoming more comfortable with exposing some of her weaknesses. She realized that friendships were all about give and take, and that her flaws would not prevent true friends from loving her. "People close to me see what I'm struggling with faster than I do because I become Trouper Neve and I say, 'Everything's fine, I'm okay,'" Neve related to *Mademoiselle*. "But I think my friends would like to see me break down once in a while and go, 'Wow, this really sucks.' I've started to in the last few months. It's my big project. To sit down with someone I'm close with and say, 'Wow, this really sucks.' And you know what? It feels really good!"

Armed with a somewhat active dating life and a more mature outlook on work and fame, Neve was beginning to appreciate the person she had grown into. She had made something incredible out of her life, and had only herself to thank for it. The knowledge of her inner strength and abilities gave Neve a fresh sense of inner calm and self-awareness. Surging with personal power, Campbell proclaimed her newfound self-reliance and happiness to *Time International*, "Happiness is a choice. I could sit here and say I'm really tired, and I work far too much, and I wish I had more time for my loved ones. Or I could sit here and say working is a great problem to have, and I have wonderful opportunities, and at some point I'll be able to take as much time off as I want. I choose to be happy."

Eleven

LIFE IS BEAUTIFUL

eve Campbell, the actress who captivated audiences with her gut-wrenching portrayals of Julia Salinger and Sidney Prescott, was now ready to show a side of herself that was only briefly unveiled during her hosting stints on *Mad TV* (Fox-TV, November 2, 1996) and *Saturday Night Live* (NBC-TV, February 8, 1997). Blessed with a great sense of humor, Campbell was weary of playing overly dramatic roles. The happiness she felt after years of struggle and deprivation required a constructive outlet. Doing screen comedy had also become imperative to her career mobility, since many of her fans were satiated with seeing Neve at her emotional worst. "I am doing [a] romantic comedy next, so I hope people will get to see another side of me," she told the *Buffalo News*. "I really want people to see me in a role where I'm not crying, I'm not screaming, and I'm not an orphan. People have to be getting tired of seeing me like that."

The roles she had selected after *Scream 2* were a major departure from her outworn big screen image. Signing up for films such as *54* (1998), *The Lion King II: Simba's Pride* (1998), *Hair Shirt* (1998), *Three to Tango* (1999), and *Panic* (2000), Neve vowed to lighten up oncamera, and, in so doing, propelled her acting career on a new, versatile track.

A Miramax production, 54 was a tribute to the late 1970s disco era. Based on the legendary Studio 54 nightclub in Manhattan and the excessive lifestyle of its notorious owner, Steve Rubell (Mike Myers), the film documented the story of New Jersey–native Shane O'Shea's (Ryan Phillippe) rise from common busboy to highly revered and well-paid bartender. As a lowly worker in the highly guarded nightclub, the young hero befriends a young couple, Greg (Breckin Meyer—who once appeared in an episode of *Party of Five* as a potential boyfriend of Julia) and Anita (Salma Hayek). He and his equally novice and impressionable pals get swept up in the club's pervasive anything-goes atmosphere. However, when Shane meets his dream girl, ambitious soap star Julie Black (Neve Campbell), he begins to question if there is such a thing as "life" outside Studio 54.

Director and writer Mark Christopher discussed the idea's inspiration and evolution with the *Hollywood Reporter*. "I grew up in Fort Dodge, Iowa, so I didn't experience Studio 54 firsthand. But through my obsession with the Disco Era, and reading everything I could get my hands on, as well as hiring the right people, I was able to recreate the 1970s experience up there on screen. 54 is a coming-of-age story about an innocent guy who becomes a bartender at the club. It was [filmmaker/screenwriter] Paul Schrader, my counselor at Columbia University film school, who suggested the story be told from a bartender's point of view."

Like many people born after the boogie era, Neve was captivated by the glamour of the 1970s. It wasn't her preoccupation with disco, however, that convinced her to accept the role of Julie Black. Instead, the decisive factor was the chance to visit her family in Toronto, where the film was to be shot. "The thing with that is that it was actually a favor for Miramax," she explained to *University Wire*. "My character's not huge in it. It's what I could do [schedule-wise] at the time of *Party of Five*. The character was a lot of fun. She was a soap opera star from the '70s who used to live in New Jersey and has chosen this other life. She is Ryan Phillippe's fantasy throughout the film. Also, the main reason I did the film was because I got to go home during the fall. I got to see the leaves change color."

Although the production was completed on time, and was even overseen by Miramax co-chairman Harvey Weinstein, the final version that made its way into theatres had very little in common with Christopher's original vision. When Miramax tested the first cut in front of audiences, the reaction was a resounding thumbs down.

To remedy the situation, many scenes were reshot and some were eliminated altogether, including a homosexual sequence in which Ryan Phillippe and Breckin Meyer kiss onscreen. In an interview with *Entertainment Weekly*, Christopher commented, "This was a very ambitious story line from the start. Our goal was to keep the audience sympathetic to the characters, [and] any material that was removed from the film was removed because it was too challenging for some members of the audience. However, I'm excited because some of the most groundbreaking material really played and still remains."

Judging by the response of fans and critics, the "groundbreaking material" was not enough to save the new release. In its opening weekend on August 30, 1998, 54 only grossed $6 million, later earning a paltry total of $16 million in the United States. While it seemed that disco was in the air in 1998, because another film on the theme, *The Last Days of Disco* opened on May 29, 1998, it had an even lower box-office gross totaling a mere $3 million. Apparently, most moviegoers were uninterested in the disco revival. Yet, unlike the scathing critical reviews garnered by 54, famed film critic Roger Ebert appraised *The Last Days of Disco* favorably. "The movie is the latest sociological romance by Whit

Stillman (*Metropolitan*, *Barcelona*), who nails his characters with perfectly heard dialogue and laconic satire."

Kenneth Turan, film reviewer for the *Los Angeles Times*, handed down this verdict for *54*: "If you've never understood why people begged, wheedled, and pleaded to get past the velvet rope and into the celebrated discos of the 1970s, don't look to *54* to enlighten you. Decadence has rarely looked so pathetic, lethargic, and dispiriting as it does in this listless film." *Entertainment Weekly* also disparaged the effort with a C rating and the following comment: "As the movie keeps telling us, Studio 54 was more than a disco. It was a world of fantasy and freedom, where everyone joined in the pulsating ritual of music, dance, ecstasy. But in *54*, we don't get to see much ecstasy. For all the fascination of its subject, the movie is flat, logy, and amateurish—a Scotch-tape-and-balsa-wood job that takes us into the fabled nightclub and then strands us, through sheer ineptitude, on the sidelines."

Luckily, Neve's minor role in *54* saved her from having to bear the responsibility for the polyester-clad disaster. Having escaped with her reputation intact, she immediately signed up for a role in Warner Bros.' lighthearted comedy *Three to Tango*. "All my characters so far have had dead parents. So maybe it's time for a comedy," she reasoned in *Time International*.

Her work on *Three to Tango* would once again bring her home to Toronto. But this time she would have a more significant screen part to call her own. From her description of the film to *TV Guide*, it was clear that Neve was excited about her latest project. "My character is having an affair with an older man [Dylan McDermott] who is a business tycoon, and he hires a young architect to build a building for him. And he believes that the young architect, Matt Perry's character, is homosexual. And he asks Matt Perry's character to spy on me to make sure that I'm faithful. And Matt

Perry's character does that. We befriend one another and he falls in love with me. All the while, I believe he's gay. So in a sense, it's like *When Harry Met Sally . . .* [1998]. It's two people who are spending a lot of time with each other on a friendship basis, but there's a sexual attraction."

The romantic comedy's *Three's Company*–shenanigans gave Neve the chance to showcase her humor and wit, as well as work alongside Matthew Perry (TV's *Friends*, *Fools Rush In*), Dylan McDermott (*Til There Was You*, TV's *The Practice*), and Oliver Platt (*Bulworth*). She would, of course, have to sharpen her comedic timing to keep up with America's funniest friend and fellow Canadian, Matthew Perry.

Neve's apprehensions were unfounded, because she was soon impressing her new costars on the set. Like most of her fans, they too were taken aback by her innate sense of humor. "I was excited about having the opportunity to work with Neve, who I think is great," Perry told the *Toronto Star*. "Now that we've been shooting, it really feels right."

The supermarket tabloids were soon hot on the actress's trail, romantically linking Campbell and her friendly costar. Her single status coupled with the public's consumptive need for gossip, fueled rumors of an affair between Matthew and Neve. Although the pair was spotted hanging out together around Toronto on numerous occasions, neither publicly confirmed the alleged relationship.

An attractive single woman, rumors about Neve's love life were bound to spread. The truth, however, was that twenty-six-year-old Neve was more interested in improving her relationship with her brother, Christian, than wasting her energy on short-term romances. Even though he was living and working in Los Angeles, her busy schedule prevented them from seeing each other as often as they would have liked. Save for one independent film (*Trick*) and several made-for-television movies (*Born to Run, Picture Perfect*), Christian wasn't getting much work since his days as Teddy on TV's *Malibu Shores* (1996). He elaborated to the *Toronto Star*, "Years ago, it was hard because I was really struggling, having a hard time even feeding myself, and then to watch her get all this fame and money—I was, like, 'What is going on? What's going on in my life?' Now I'm finding my own place."

Part of Christian's healing process involved starting the Blue Sphere Alliance, a theatre company based in Los Angeles. While Neve was excited about the venture, even offering to help out in her off time, she quickly discovered how few spare moments she actually had to invest. That realization made her feel she was letting her brother down. As she told the *Mr. Showbiz* Web site, "I have to be very careful of spreading myself too thin right now because I'm working so much."

When Christian suggested starting their own production team and working on a new movie featuring friends from Canada, his famous sister was all encouragement from the start. As she placed more emphasis on her personal life and renewed her commitment to spend more quality time with Christian, she decided that working with her brother would be the perfect way to accomplish both goals. "We're very similar," Neve told *Australian Hits*. "My brother and I are both very focused and we always have been, and determined. My brother's a wonderful, wonderful person. He's probably my best friend in the whole world and we're extremely close. So, I think that's probably why there's a lot of resemblance in our work."

Hair Shirt (1998) would not only bring Neve and Christian closer together, it would also give her the chance to produce a project, an idea she had been toying with for years. While most actors have to wait until their elder years of popularity to get their production efforts green-lighted, Neve's meteoric rise to fame considerably diminished that waiting period. She had conquered both television and films, and was now set to make her mark in a behind-the-scenes capacity. Always seeking out the next career challenge, she wasn't content unless she was trying something new. "Christian and I had been wanting to produce for a while," she told the *Toronto Star*. "We'd gone to a Martin Scorsese tribute in L.A. a couple of years ago, and realized that the same people had worked basically in all of his movies—he kept his movie family very, very tight. And we have this pool of talented friends who we really believe in, and I'm in a position where I can create that, so why not? Why not bring all these people together and create something?"

When Christian's friends (writers Dean Paras, Katie Wright, and Nate Tuck) collaborated on the screenplay, they had no idea it would one day become a feature film. "I conceived the idea over a weekend," Paras told the *Toronto Star*, "and then we said, 'Let's take a road trip and hammer it out.' So we (girlfriend Katie Wright, pal Nate Tuck) drove here to Toronto, discussing the movie and how to make it work. We were thinking it was just a piece of cake and we were crazy."

Hair Shirt chronicles the misadventures of a neurotic, young womanizer named Danny Reilly (Dean Paras). Neve plays a Hollywood diva named Renee Weber, one of his past conquests. She is determined to have her revenge when she discovers that her old flame is carrying the torch for another actress, Corey Wells (Katie Wright). A fun romantic comedy about adapting to life in the Los Angeles fast lane, the release scored points for a tight ensemble effort and an interesting premise.

Although she only had time to make a small appearance in the project, Neve worried that people would confuse her with the obnoxious movie star she depicted in the film. "I had a bit of apprehension that people would make the assumption that that's actually me, because she is a television and film star," she said to the *Toronto Star*. "But I played the role so extreme and it's such a comedic role that I'm hoping people don't make that assumption. I think in the press I'm a very honest person, and people don't think of me like that."

Prior to making *Hair Shirt*, the production biz was completely foreign to Neve and her cohorts. Except for what Neve had absorbed through *Party of Five* and her film work, the group was pretty much on their own when it came to learning the ropes. Rather than treating her ignorance of the filmmaking business as a liability, she perceived it as a benefit. "It was definitely a lot more work than we had imagined," she told the *Toronto Sun*, "and it offered a huge amount of challenges. But, on the other hand, it was an amazing experience. I think because we were all new at it there was a great amount of enthusiasm. For me it was like going to film school for four years. We had a lot of creative control and we were able to help each other out. We were all very humbled by the experience and realized that we were all learning. It was a team effort."

The film completed, Neve and her team prepared to submit *Hair Shirt* to movie festivals. The process was much like applying to college, their first choice being the prestigious Toronto Film Festival. With their fingers crossed, the Canadian friends hoped that they could return to Canada with their own project on the festival lineup. Their mission was soon accomplished. The Toronto Film Festival invited them to screen their entry on September 12, 1998. Neve spoke for the whole group when she told the *Toronto Star*, "I love this city, I'm very proud to be a Torontonian and to be able to premiere the film here in front of our friends and family, and everyone's so enthusiastic, it's fantastic."

Although the film did not receive positive reviews (a critic for the Web site Jam! Movies called it "a standard romantic comedy that's been done to death"), the feature showed Campbell what it felt like to be on the other side of the camera; an understanding that will, no doubt, become useful as her acting career progresses.

All of a sudden, Neve found herself addicted to the surge of power she'd felt while making *Hair Shirt*. The control and freedom was like a drug that left her yearning for another "fix." The concept that she could create something concrete out of an idea was inspiring for the young artist. "I love it!" Campbell exclaimed to the *Toronto Star*. "It was so nice to have more creative control on a project as opposed to just being a puppet, and showing up and doing the lines. It was more about calling the shots."

Helping her friends secure work was also a highly appealing prospect. Her decision to produce wasn't solely philanthropic. Like most Hollywood actresses, Neve was frustrated with the scarcity of good roles available for women. Producing would give her the chance to establish a more equal playing ground. "If there aren't a lot of female projects out there," she told *Time International*, "then I'll create them."

The timing for launching her career as a producer was perfect. Movie studios were desperate to get the better-known television stars into films and dangled lucrative production deals as bait. Jennifer Love Hewitt, for example, was one such star who could wield the type of power that used to be reserved for more seasoned actors. One night, after a visionary dream, Hewitt woke up with a film idea in her head. *Marry Me Jane* (1999) was a romantic teenage comedy—just what the studios were looking for. So Hewitt jotted down the concept and sold it to New Line Cinema for $500,000. "I woke up from a romantic dream and I was like, 'That was nice and I want to share this dream with people,'" she elaborated to *USA Today*. "I wrote it down and made a ten-page treatment, I had never written one before. Then I put on the business suit and went into ten or fifteen studio offices in L.A. and said, 'Forget I am Jennifer Love Hewitt for the forty-five minutes that I am here, and let me tell you this story and see if you like it.' When I think about it, I know any day now they are going to call and say 'Ha ha, big joke on you!' but I am really excited."

Matthew Lillard, Neve's former boyfriend and costar, was making the most of similar opportunities with *Spanish Judges* (1999), a film that cost $3.5 million to make. "Our generation is really aggressive," he informed *Entertainment Weekly*, "and Hollywood gives more and more power to younger people, so we just took advantage of it."

There are many more young stars/producers where Neve, Hewitt, and Lillard came from. Drew Barrymore (*Ever After*, *Home Fries*) produced the comedy *Never Been Kissed* (1999), and David Arquette (*Scream*, *Scream 2*) co-produced the drama *Dream with the Fishes* (1997). More recently, Jerry O'Connell (*Jerry Maguire*, *Scream 2*) wrote and sold his first script, *First Daughter*, to New Regency Pictures.

Seeing the fervid industry of her peers, Neve indicated to her agent at Creative Artists Agency that she too would be receptive to a production deal. She had only to say the word. "The wonderful thing is I've now got studios coming to me and saying, 'Would you like to develop something? Do you have a story that you'd like to tell? What would you like to try?'" Neve told *TV Guide*. "And you can't ask for a better position than that. So now it's coming up with the ideas and reading some great books and going with that. And that's a fantastic position to be in. And I think that this industry is changing in that way, where the studios are having more respect for women and allowing them to develop stories. Hey, if I have the opportunity, I might as well take it."

The only question now was what project to make. Neve racked her mind for concepts and story ideas. But after plowing through books, magazines, and newspapers for inspiration, she was as confused as ever, if not more so. It was then that she decided to look to herself for the answer. Reflecting back on her life and all her past experiences, Neve realized that a passion for dance was something she would never part with. She decided that blending the worlds of film and dance would be her next mission. "I would love to incorporate my dance into something, be it a film or TV project, or go back to the theater," Neve confided in *UniverCity*. "It's a tough one though . . . musicals aren't as popular now as they once were. I was born in the wrong generation. I should have been born when Gene Kelly, Fred Astaire and Ginger Rogers were making movies—that's when I was supposed to be a movie star."

Neve wouldn't have to wait long to make her *Move* (2000). When producers Ben Myron, Alan Riche, and Tony Ludwig learned Neve was contemplating bringing dance back to the big screen, they immediately brought a film idea to her, requesting that writer Eric Guggenheim (*Wetworks*, *Trim*) collaborate with her on the script. The film was sold to Warner Bros. and is slated to go into production in the summer of 1999.

Besides a starring role and the contribution of her own dance experiences to the story, Neve plans to co-produce the movie venture. "The dance world is very masochistic, which is what I want to show in the movie," she elaborated to *Jane* magazine. "You see this incredible beauty and grace on the stage, and then backstage you see the pain."

Move documents the life of a classical ballet dancer (Neve), who comes to New York to pursue her dream. When she is confronted by two opposing dance teachers, the young dancer finds that she must choose between the restrictive but safe world of ballet and the exhilarating but unstable environment of a modern dance troupe. The film features a contemporary soundtrack and energetic choreography, reminiscent of such classic dance films as *Fame* (1980), *Flashdance* (1983), and *Dirty Dancing* (1987).

Also on Neve's slate of forthcoming big screen projects is the comedy *Drowning Mona* (2000), produced by Neverland Films and Jersey Shore. This comedy, written by Peter Steinfeld, is to be directed by Nick Gomez and costars Bette Midler, Danny DeVito, and Jamie Lee Curtis.

The take-charge approach Neve has used in her career is paying off. She is securing the acting roles she wants and is being given more control than she could ever have anticipated. For Campbell, however, control isn't so much about bullying people into submission as it is about carefully guiding her career in the right direction. That's why when Miramax Films tried to persuade her to do *Scream* 3 (1999), Neve resisted the temptation, at least at first. Miramax was willing to go to any length to secure Neve's cooperation, including making a role (which eventually went to Gretchen Mol) that she wanted in *Rounders* (1998) with Matt Damon contingent on her involvement, and offering her approximately $5 million for reprising the role of Sidney. She made it clear, however, that her participation in *Scream* 3 was not up for sale. "They've offered close to $5 million for *Scream* 3," she told the Massachusettes based *Patriot Ledger*, "but, so far, I haven't agreed. I don't want to do it on my next hiatus if it's the only movie I can do. It's not that I'm bargaining for more money. I just want to do something different."

Worried that a third turn as Sidney Prescott would categorize her permanently as a scream queen, Neve didn't want to jump the gun. "They'd really like me to say, 'Yes I'll do it now.' Because they need to write the script," she explained to *University Wire*. "But I don't want to be typecast as Sidney or Julia and I only get the opportunity to do one movie on my hiatus. If I find another really fantastic script, and it's a choice between *Scream* 3 and this other script, I'll do the other script. I could make a *Scream* 3 and everyone will see me and it'll be successful, but people might think that's all I can do again and I won't have a career after that. Then what do I want to choose? Do I want to choose a lot of money or do I want to choose longevity?"

The opportunity to evaluate the script's quality before signing on was important to Neve. The risk of being pigeonholed was just too great. If she was going to do the entry, the script would have to be even more clever and shocking than its predecessors. Yet Kevin Williamson, meanwhile, harbored no doubts that his latest attempt would be a triumph. Confident that *Scream 3* would blow the skeptics away, the scribe was hyping his latest effort even before it was completed. "The theme of the first movie was, 'Don't blame the movies.' The theme of *Scream 2* was, 'We'll show you who to blame,'" he revealed to *Sci-Fi* magazine. "It starts in the home. It all starts in the mind. And *Scream 3* continues the theme to the next level."

On March 1, 1999, Neve announced that she would indeed be returning to the screen in *Scream 3*. Coming to this decision wasn't easy, but it may have been a result of her continued friendship with director Wes Craven. He had gone so far as to tell Miramax that he wouldn't do the picture unless she was a part of the package. Much like her commitments to *Party of Five* and *Hair Shirt*, signing on for *Scream 3* was another indication of Campbell's loyalty to the people she cared for. Neve showed that no matter how famous, rich, or powerful she had become, friendships would always come first.

THE FUTURE AWAITS

eve Campbell has come a long way since her days of modeling underwear in 1991. A major box-office draw as the twenty-first century begins, the actress now holds one of the most powerful positions in Hollywood, alongside such actresses as Drew Barrymore, Jennifer Love Hewitt, Jennifer Lopez, and Claire Danes. In a matter of five years, Neve has gone from taking on minor roles in such obscure movies as *Paint Cans* (1994) and *The Dark* (1994), to being offered to produce feature films *(Move)* by major Hollywood studios. She has shown just how far strategic career planning and good instincts can take you.

All the while, the *Party of Five* TV series demanded her time and attention. Just like Campbell herself, her onscreen alter ego Julia Salinger, a role model for young women all over the world, has coped with her own fair share of life-changing transitions. The character that started as an awkward, insecure teen during the first and second season has gone on to marry, divorce, and cope with a boyfriend's abuse in the third, fourth, and fifth seasons respectively. Yet, as all good things must end, so will her six-year contract with the series. Exhausted with balancing her small and big-screen responsibilities, Neve is anxiously looking forward to being released from her contractual obligations. "April 2000, and then I'll have a life and take time off whenever I want, and do movies if I want," she confided to *Jane* magazine in May 1999. "I am completely loyal to the show, I am; but any job, if you've been doing it for a while, can become monotonous. I've been playing the same character for the last five years."

Having recently bought her mother a home only half a mile from her own in Brentwood, California, Neve has made it clear that family will play a major part in the new "life" she envisions. Christian, now in his later twenties, is still busy acting in Los Angeles, and her teenage half-brother Damian has decided to make Los Angeles his home base to work as a Web site designer.

Now, with a tight-knit family around her, Neve feels much more at home in Los Angeles. Recently, she has been romantically linked with thirty-something actor John Cusack (*The Grifters*, *Pushing Tin*). It seems that Neve is at long last coming to grips with the course her life has taken. "I've got a lot to love about my life," she revealed to *Jane* magazine. "I'm lucky enough to have a job that I love—not many people have that. I love that I have enough money not to worry about money, and to be able to help my family and friends."

Over the centuries, there have been many tales of triumph over adversity. But never has a story been portrayed so eloquently and poignantly than by Neve Campbell's incredible rise to show-business fame. With the roots of her success planted both in her strong-willed character and her troubled childhood, she is truly a role model for her generation. But it's not because she has played the morally sound Julia Salinger on *Party of Five*, nor is it because she has remained true to her beliefs in the face of immense opposition. No, Neve's life story is moving because she has, without so much as breaking a rule or hurting anyone intentionally, managed to steer clear of every Hollywood pitfall. Through it all, her strong convictions have helped her avoid falling prey to Hollywood's three deadliest sins: glory, vanity, and greed.

In the myriad of comments and descriptions offered over the years by Neve's friends and associates, one voice has revealed best who she really is and continually strives to be. In an interview with *Entertainment Weekly*, filmmaker Wes Craven spoke candidly, saying, "There's just no bullshit about Neve. She's the exact opposite of the actress who has to run to her trailer every five minutes because her makeup's not right. She's got a real sense of what's important in life and has everything in perspective."

Endowed with an incredible range of emotion, talent, and acting abilities, Neve Campbell is one actress who seems destined to overcome every personal and professional obstacle that could stand in her way. No one knows what the future holds, but if the past is any indication, Neve's success is bound to endure.

NEVE CAMPBELL FILMOGRAPHY

Feature Films

THE DARK

(1994, IMPERIAL ENTERTAINMENT) 87 MINUTES, R

PRODUCERS: Robert Bergman and Craig Pryce

DIRECTOR: Craig Pryce

WRITER: Robert Cooper

CAST: Stephen McHattie [Hunter], Scott Wickware [Carl Miller], Brion James [Buckner], Desmond Campbell [FBI Agent], Dennis O'Connor [Jake], Jaimz Woolvett [Ed], Cynthia Belliveau [Tracy], **Neve Campbell** [Jesse Donovan], Christopher Bondy [Gabe], William Lynn [Arnold], Bruce Beaton [Biker], Addison Bell [Al, the cook], Robbie Rox and Ian MacDonald [Bikers]

PAINT CANS

(1994, SALTER STREET FILMS) 100 MINUTES, UNRATED

PRODUCERS: Paul Donovan, Alan MacGillivray, Mike Mahoney, and Benedict O'Halloran

DIRECTOR: Paul Donovan

WRITER: Paul Donovan

CAST: Chas Lawther [Wick Burns], Martha Burns [Melda], Bruce

Greenwood [Vittorio Musso], Andy Jones [Neville Lewis], Paul Gross [Morton Ridgewell], Anne-Marie MacDonald [Inge Von Nerthus], **Neve Campbell** [Tristesse], Kelly-Ruth Mercier [Tamanee], Jennie Overton [Anna], Jim Swansburg [Waiter], Don Francks [Maitland Burns], Lex Gigeroff [Oliver], Shelley Wenaus [Morgan Musso], Adam Westerback [Tartufo], Robyn Stevan [Arundel Merton], Alan MacGillivray [Harold Meade]

BAREE (A.K.A. *NORTHERN PASSAGE*)

(1994, TRIMARK PICTURES) 96 MINUTES, PG-13

PRODUCERS: Christian Charret, Justine Héroux, Séverine Olivier-Lacamp, Robert Réa, and Jacques Salles

DIRECTOR: Arnaud Sélignac

WRITERS: James Oliver Curwood, Jonathan Hales (based on the novel by Curwood)

CAST: Jeff Fahey [Paul], Jacques Weber [Pierre], Lorne Brass [Taggart], **Neve Campbell** [Nepeese], Geneviève Rochette [Marie], Billy Two Rivers [Broken Foot]

LOVE CHILD

(1995, INDEPENDENT) 23 MINUTES, UNRATED

PRODUCER: Patrick Sisam

DIRECTOR: Patrick Sisam

WRITER: Patrick Sisam

CAST: Dov Tiefenbach [Murray], **Neve Campbell** [Deidre], Cecilley Carroll [Nancy]

THE CRAFT

(1996, COLUMBIA PICTURES) 101 MINUTES, R

PRODUCERS: Ginny Nugent and Douglas Wick

DIRECTOR: Andrew Fleming

WRITERS: Peter Filardi and Andrew Fleming

CAST: Robin Tunney [Sarah Bailey], Fairuza Balk [Nancy Downs], **Neve Campbell** [Bonnie], Rachel True [Rochelle], Skeet Ulrich [Chris], Christine Taylor [Laura Lizzie], Breckin Meyer [Mitt], Nathaniel Marston [Trey], Cliff De Young [Mr. Bailey], Assumpta Serna [Lirio], Helen Shaver [Grace], Janet E. Eilber (Sarah's Mother)

SCREAM

(1996, DIMENSION FILMS) 111 MINUTES, R
PRODUCERS: Stuart M. Besser, J. Capp, Cathy Konrad, Marianne Maddalena, Nicholas Mastandrea, Bob Weinstein, Harvey Weinstein, and Cary Woods
DIRECTOR: Wes Craven
WRITER: Kevin Williamson
CAST: David Arquette [Deputy Dwight Riley], **Neve Campbell** [Sidney Prescott], Courteney Cox [Gale Weathers], Kevin Patrick Walls [Steven Orith], Jamie Kennedy [Randy Meeks], David Booth [Casey's Father], Matthew Lillard [Stuart Macher], Carla Hatley [Casey's Mother], Rose McGowan [Tatum Riley], Skeet Ulrich [Billy Loomis], Drew Barrymore [Casey Becker], Lawrence Hecht [Neil Prescott], Liev Schreiber [Cotton Weary], W. Earl Brown [Kenny, the cameraman], Joseph Whipp [Sheriff Burke], Lois Saunders [Mrs. Tate]

SCREAM 2

(1997, DIMENSION FILMS) 116 MINUTES, R
PRODUCERS: Cary Granat, Cathy Konrad, Daniel Lupi, Marianne Maddalena, Nicholas Mastandrea, Julie Plec, Richard Potter, Andrew Rona, Bob Weinstein, Harvey Weinstein, and Kevin Williamson
DIRECTOR: Wes Craven
WRITER: Kevin Williamson

CAST: David Arquette [Dwight "Dewey" Riley], **Neve Campbell** [Sidney Prescott], Courteney Cox [Gale Weathers], Sarah Michelle Gellar [Casey "Cici" Cooper], Jamie Kennedy [Randy Meeks], Duane Martin [Joel, the cameraman], Laurie Metcalf [Reporter Debbie Salt], Elise Neal [Hallie], Jerry O'Connell [Derek], Timothy Olyphant [Mickey], Jada Pinkett [Maureen Evans], Liev Schreiber [Cotton Weary], Lewis Arquette [Chief Louis Hartley], Rebecca Gayheart [Sorority Sister Lois], Portia de Rossi [Sorority Sister Murphy]

THE LION KING II: SIMBA'S PRIDE

(1998, WALT DISNEY PICTURES) 75 MINUTES, G

PRODUCER: Jeannine Roussel

DIRECTORS: Rob LaDuca and Darrell Rooney

WRITERS: Jonathan Cuba, Flip Kobler, Cindy Marcus, Mark McCorkle, Bill Motz, Gregory Poirier, Bob Roth, Robert Schooley, Linda Voorhees, and Jenny Wingfield

CAST (VOICES): Matthew Broderick [Simba], **Neve Campbell** [Kiara], Andy Dick [Nuka], Robert Guillaume [Rafiki], James Earl Jones [Mufasa], Moira Kelly [Nala], Nathan Lane [Timon], Jason Marsden [Kovu], Suzanne Pleshette [Zira], Ernie Sabella [Pumbaa]

WILD THINGS

(1998, MANDALAY ENTERTAINMENT) 107 MINUTES, R

PRODUCERS: Kevin Bacon, Steven Brown, Steven A. Jones, Rodney M. Liber, Scott R. Price, and Suzy Sachs

DIRECTOR: John McNaughton

WRITER: Stephen Peters

CAST: Kevin Bacon [Ray Duquette], Matt Dillon [Sam Lombardo], **Neve Campbell** [Suzie Toller], Theresa Russell [Sandra Van Ryan], Denise Richards [Kelly Van Ryan], Daphne Rubin-Vega

[Gloria Perez], Robert Wagner [Tom Baxter], Bill Murray [Ken Bowden], Carrie Snodgress [Ruby], Jeff Perry [Bryce Hunter], Cory Pendergast [Jimmy Leach], Toi Svane [Nicole]

HAIR SHIRT

(1998, LUNATIC PRODUCTIONS) 91 MINUTES, UNRATED
PRODUCERS: Christian Campbell, Neve Campbell, Dean Paras, Nate Tuck, Elizabeth Weber, and Katie Wright
DIRECTOR: Dean Paras
WRITERS: Dean Paras, Nate Tuck, and Katie Wright
CAST: Dean Paras [Danny Reilly], Katie Wright [Corey Wells], **Neve Campbell** [Renee Weber], Kimberly Huie [Kimberly], Stefan Brogren [Tim], David DeLuise [Peter Angelo], Rebecca Gayheart [Jennifer], and: Christian Campbell, Adam Carolla

54

(1998, MIRAMAX FILMS) 89 MINUTES, R
PRODUCERS: Don Carmody, Bobby Cohen, Ira Deutchman, Richard N. Gladstein, Dolly Hall, Jonathan King, Bob Weinstein, and Harvey Weinstein
DIRECTOR: Mark Christopher
WRITER: Mark Christopher
CAST: Ryan Phillippe [Shane O'Shea], Salma Hayek [Anita], Sela Ward [Billie Auster], Breckin Meyer [Greg Randazzo], Sherry Stringfield [Viv], **Neve Campbell** [Julie Black], Mike Myers [Steve Rubell], Heather Matarazzo [Grace O'Shea], Ellen Albertini Dow [Disco Dottie], Skipp Sudduth [Harlan O'Shea], Jay Goelde [Buck], Jason Andrews [Anthony], Lorri Bagley [Patti], Mark Ruffilo [Richie]

THREE TO TANGO

(1999, WARNER BROS.) PG-13

PRODUCERS: Lawrence Abramson, Robert F. Newmyer, Jeffrey Silver, and Bettina Sofia Viviano
DIRECTOR: Damon Santostefano
WRITERS: Alene Brosh McKenna and Rodney Patrick Vaccaro
CAST: Matthew Perry [Oscar], **Neve Campbell** [Amy], Dylan McDermott [Charles Newman], Oliver Platt [Peter Steinberg], and Cylk Cosart, Bob Balaban [Strous], John C. McGinley [Decker], Kelly Rowan

---

Television Films

I KNOW MY SON IS ALIVE (A.K.A. WEB OF DECEIT)

(1994, NBC-TV) 120 MINUTES, UNRATED
PRODUCERS: Les Alexander, Joseph Broido, Don Enright, and Julian Marks
DIRECTOR: Bill Corcoran
WRITERS: Joseph Broido and Raymond Hartung
CAST: Corbin Bernsen [Mark], Amanda Pays [Katherine], Al Waxman [Herb], Mimi Kuzyk [Laura], **Neve Campbell** [Beth], Tom McCamus [Falcone], Kim Coates [Detective Griffi], Albert Schultz [Bernie], Nigel Bennett [Eisner], Carlton Watson [Detective Gaffey], Peter Krantz [Scott], Helen Beavis [Mrs. Lassell], Caroline Yeager [Bank Teller], David Berni [Young Cop]

JANEK: THE FORGET-ME-NOT MURDERS

(1994, CBS-TV) 120 MINUTES, UNRATED
PRODUCERS: Robert "Buzz" Berger, Robert Iscove, and Marilyn Stonehouse
DIRECTOR: Robert Iscove
WRITER: Gerald DiPego (based on the novel by William Bayer)
CAST: Richard Crenna [Frank Janek], Tyne Daly [Dr. Archer], Cliff Gorman [Aaron], Philip Bosco [Chief], Diane D'Aquila [Alexis],

John Vernon [Boyce], Helen Shaver [Monique], Angel David [Leo Titus], Michael Genet [Agent Tapper], **Neve Campbell** [Jess Foy], Marcia Bennett [Laura Foy], Amber Lea Weston [Fran], Yannick Bisson [Greg Gale], Dean McDermott [Agent Alex], Heidi Hatashita [Agent Kay], Shelley Cook [Diane Proctor]

THE CANTERVILLE GHOST

(1996, ABC-TV) 92 MINUTES, PG

PRODUCERS: Robert Benedetti, Malcolm J. Christopher, Brent Shields, Patrick Stewart, and Richard Welsh

DIRECTOR: Sydney Macartney

WRITERS: Robert Benedetti (based on the play by Oscar Wilde)

CAST: Patrick Stewart [Sir Simon de Canterville], **Neve Campbell** [Ginny Otis], Joan Sims [Mrs. Umney], Donald Sinden [Mr. Umney], Cherie Lunghi [Lucille Otis], Edward Wiley [Hiram Otis], Leslie Phillips [George, Lord Canterville], Daniel Betts [Francis, Duke of Cheshire], Ciarán Fitzgerald [Adam Otis], Raymond Pickard [Washington Otis]

Television Series

CATWALK

(1992–94, YTV [CANADA]; SYNDICATED/MTV [USA]) 60 MINUTES, UNRATED

PRODUCERS: Tab Baird and Wendy Grean

DIRECTORS: Jerry Ciccoritti, Steve DiMarco, Ken Girotti and Eleanor Lindo

CAST: Lisa Butler [Sierra Williams], **Neve Campbell** [Daisy McKenzie], Christopher Lee Clements [Atlas Robinson], Keram Malicki-Sánchez [Johnnie Camden], Paul Popowich [Jesse Carlson], Kelli Taylor [Mary Owens]

PARTY OF FIVE

(1994–PRESENT, FOX-TV) 60 MINUTES, UNRATED

PRODUCERS: Michael Engler, Susannah Grant, Valerie Joseph, Christopher Keyser, Amy Lippman, Paul Marks, Lisa Melamed, Bruce J. Nachbar, John Romano, P. K. Simonds, Ken Topolsky

DIRECTORS: Lou Antonio, Daniel Attias, Arwin Brown, et al.

CAST: Scott Wolf [Bailey Salinger], Matthew Fox [Charlie Salinger], Neve Campbell [Julia Salinger Holbrook], Lacey Chabert [Claudia Salinger], Paula Devicq [Kirsten Bennett], Jennifer Love Hewitt [Sarah Reeves], Alexondra Lee [Callie Martel], Jeremy London [Griffin Holbrook], Michael Goorjian [Justin Thompson], Scott Grimes [Will McCorkle], Zachary and Alexander Ahnert, then Brandon and Taylor Porter, then Steven and Andrew Cavarno, then later Jacob Smith [Owen Salinger]

NEVE CAMPBELL ONLINE

Campbell's Corner
www.free.prohosting.com/scream67/index.html

The Danish Neve Campbell Page
www.nevecampbell.dk/

Neve Campbell
www.geocities.com/Hollywood/Set/4114/neve.htm

Neve Campbell
www.geocities.com/SunsetStrip/Stage/7212/Neve.html

Neve Campbell by Ppm
www.chez.com/neve/indexus.html

Neve Campbell dot org
www.nevecampbell.org

Neve Campbell Online
www.neveonline.com

Neve Campbell Online
www.geocities.com/Hollywood/Studio/6575/

The Neve Campbell Page
www.ionet.net/~zkeas/

Neve Campbell—Poetry in Motion
www1.tip.nl/~t461078/neve/neve.htm

Neve Campbell—Very Nice
www.geocities.com/Hollywood/Lot/7885/NEVE.HTM

The Neve Campbell Web Domain
www.geocities.com/Hollywood/Cinema/5565/

Yet Another Neve Campbell Shrine
www.iaw.on.ca/~bjmac/

Bibliography

Adilman, Sid. "Partying till Dawn on the Set of *Three to Tango*," *Toronto Star*, June 26, 1998.

"Any Witch Way She Can." *Australian TV Week*, August 1997.

Arnold, Chuck. "Chatter." *People*, October 27, 1997, p. 120.

Ascher-Walsh, Rebecca. "The 411 on 54." *Entertainment Weekly*, September 4, 1998, pp. 20–23.

Ascher-Walsh, Rebecca, Kristen Baldwin, Carrie Bell, Connie Benesch, Judy Brennan, David Browne, and Rob Brun. "The It List/TV." *Entertainment Weekly*, June 27, 1997, p. 66.

Beachy, Susan Campbell and Craig Modderno. "Listen Up: Neve Campbell." *TV Guide Online* (www.tvguide.com), December 5, 1996.

Beck, Marilyn and Stacy Jenel Smith. "Budding Actress Campbell Wants to Go Back in Time." *Los Angeles Daily News*, June 3, 1998.

_____. "TV Youngbloods Infuse Hollywood." *New York Daily News*, August 9, 1998, pp. 6–7.

Beller, Miles. "Review: *The Canterville Ghost*." *Hollywood Reporter*, January 29, 1998, pp. 12, 20.

Bernstein, Abbie. "Review: *The Craft*." *Drama-Logue*, May 16, 1996, p. 32.

"The Best Television of 1995." *Time*, December 20, 1995.

Brennan, Judy. "*The Craft* Has the Knack for Scaring Up an Audience." *Los Angeles Times*, May 6, 1996, p. F1.

Bryson, Jodi. "Neve Campbell." *Sassy*, June 1996.

Bystedt, Karen Hardy. *Before They Were Stars: In Their Own Words*. Santa Monica, CA: General Publishing Group, 1996, p. 154–57.

Cerone, Daniel Howard. "Campbell's Coup." *TV Guide*, February 8, 1997, pp. 22–28.

_____. "It's My Party…and I'll Scream If I Want To!" *Australian TV Week*, March 1997.

Chance, Jack. "Why the Scream Queen May Not Be Back for 3." E! Online (www.eonline.com), December,1997.

Cohen, David. "A Walk on the Wild Side." *Jerusalem Post*, July 23, 1998, p. 11.

Cooney, Jenny. "Cursed!" *Australian TV Week*, June 15, 1997.

Corliss, Richard. "The Class of '98." *Time*, August 3, 1998, p. 66.

_____. "Swamp Sweat." *Time*, March 23, 1998, p. 79.

"A Cranky Old Ghost." *USA Today*, January 25, 1996.

Dargis, Manohla. "With a Star Turn in Scream, Life's More than a 'Party of Five.'" *US*, February 1997, p. 70.

Diamond, Jamie. "Why Neve Isn't Screaming." *Mademoiselle*, September 1998.

Dixon, Paula. "Wild Plot Wild Cast—*Wild Things*." *University Wire*, March 19, 1998.

Dunn, Jancee. "Neve Campbell." *Rolling Stone*, September 18, 1997, p. 56.

Eller, Claudia. "Word of Mouth." *Los Angeles Times*, December 12, 1997, pp. D3–D4.

Epstein, Jeffrey. "Life's a Scream." *Soap Opera Magazine*, February 11, 1997, p. 41.

Esterly, Glenn. "Party Girl." *TV Guide*, June 17, 1995, pp. 15–19.

Farley, Christopher John. "The Call of the Wild." *Time*, March 23, 1998, p. 78.

———. "Wild Thing Neve Campbell Sizzles in a New Movie and Gets Ready for a Jump to Full-time Movie Stardom." *Time*, March 30, 1998, p. 44.

Fay, Jeanne. "On the Edge." *Buzz*, January 1998, pp. 39–42.

Fleming, Michael. "Neve Campbell on Her Toes in *Move*." *Variety*, January 5, 1999, p. 5.

French, Lawrence. "Neve Campbell, No Scream Queen." *Femme Fatale*, March 1997, pp. 12–15.

Frym, Michael. "Review: *Catwalk*." *Daily Variety*, October 2, 1992.

Gennusa, Chris R. "Welcome to the Party!" *Hollywood Reporter*, August 28, 1998, pp. S1–S3.

Gerstel, Judy. "Campbells Are Up and Coming." *Toronto Star*, September 14, 1998.

Gleiberman, Owen. "The Lust Waltz in *Wild Things*." *Entertainment Weekly*, March 27, 1998, p. 46.

———. "The Velvet Mope." *Entertainment Weekly*, September 4, 1998, pp. 49–50.

Goldberg, Gabriel J. P. "Neve Campbell: Party of One." *Genre*, May 1996.

Goldman, Steven. "Full Scream Ahead!" *Interview*, January 1997, pp. 60–62.

Hedegaard, Erik. "Neve Campbell." *Detour*, March 1998.

Hobson, Louis. "Campbell's Cookin'." *Calgary Sun*, March 15, 1998.

———. "Neve Campbell Is Having a Real Scream." *Calgary Sun*, December 2, 1997.

Hochman, David. "Scream and Scream Again." *Entertainment Weekly*, November 28, 1997, p. 28.

Hofler, Robert. "Star Track." *Miami Herald*, March 27, 1998.

_____. "Who's Who in Horror?" *Los Angeles Times*, September 9, 1998, pp. F5–F7.

Hope, Darrell L. "Neve Campbell: Bewitching Hollywood Her Way." *Venice*, May 1996, p. 10.

Jewel, Dan and Anne-Marie Otey. "Reigning Canadian: At 22, *Party of Five* Star Neve Campbell Graduates to the Big Time." *People*, May 27, 1996, pp. 79–80.

Karger, Dave. "Women on the Verge: Neve Gonna Get It." *Entertainment Weekly*, June 21, 1996, p. 24.

Kelly, Brendan. "Review: Hair Shirt." *Daily Variety*, October 21, 1998, p. 44.

Kilkelly, Ned. "Welcome Back to His Nightmare." *Los Angeles Daily News*, September 28, 1996, pp. 3–4.

Kirkland, Bruce. "Pals Proudly Wear Hair Shirt." *Toronto Sun*, September 14, 1998.

Kit, Zorianna. "Career Opportunities." *Hollywood Reporter*, November 11, 1998, p. S17.

_____. "Miramax Will *Scream* Again for the Holidays." *Hollywood Reporter*, circa February 1999, p. 4.

Koltnow, Barry. "The Party Has Just Begun." *Buffalo News*, April 4, 1998.

Krantz, Michael. "Scream King." *News and Observer*, December 21, 1997.

Kronke, David. "'Five' and '2'—It Adds Up." *Los Angeles Times*, December 7, 1997, pp. 5, 46–69.

_____. "*Party* Leads to Other Invitations." *Los Angeles Times*, December 7, 1997, p. 49.

Longsdorf, Amy. "Spotlight on Neve Campbell." *Allentown Morning Call*, March 14, 1998.

Mangels, Andy. "Scream King." *Sci-Fi Universe*, December 1998, pp. 69–74.

"Meet the Party Girls." *Tiger Beat*, August 1995, pp. 86–87.

Mendelsohn, Jennifer. "Sexy, Successful—and 24." *USA Weekend,* December 14, 1997, p. 10.

Min, Janice, Monica Rizzo, and Paula Yoo. "Party Time." *People,* March 3, 1997, pp. 78–87.

Moore, Roger. "It's Her Party." *Star Watch,* January 1, 1997, p. S1.

Morales, Juan. "Neve Campbell." *Detour,* November 1996.

Murray, Steve. "Shooting the Sequel: *Scream* Machine." *Atlanta Journal and Constitution,* June 26, 1997, p. G01.

Nashawaty, Chris. "Oh, The Horror!" *Entertainment Weekly,* January 17, 1997, p. 8.

———. "*Scream* On." *Entertainment Weekly,* July 11, 1997, pp. 6–7.

———. "*Scream* on with a Surprise Hit—and Shouts for More. Wes Craven Pursues a Recurring Nightmare." *Entertainment Weekly,* July 11, 1997, p. 6.

———. "Teen Steam Sparked by a Sexy New Brat Pack." *Entertainment Weekly,* November 14, 1997, p. 24.

"Neve Campbell." *Sassy,* circa 1997.

"Neve Campbell Shares the Screen with Some of the Cutest Guys on TV—and She's Still the Life of the Party." *Soap Opera Digest,* January 30, 1996, pp. 54–56.

"The Neve You Never Knew." *Twist,* December 1998.

Noguera, Anthony. "The Dream Girl Next Door." *FHM,* June 1998.

"Party of Five." *USA Today,* November 11, 1998.

Pearlman, Cindy. "Campbell Stirs It Up with Her *Wild* New Role." *Chicago Sun-Times,* January 9, 1998.

Portman, Jamie. "An Oasis amid Chaos." *Ottawa Citizen,* December 11, 1997.

"Pumping Irony." Ireland Film and Television Network, June 17, 1998.

"Queen of the Party." *Australian TV Hits,* March 8, 1998.

Raso, Anne. "Neve's Witching Hour." *Australian Star*, November 1996.

Rebello, Stephen. "One Hundred Percent from the Heart." *Movieline*, November 1998, p. 42.

Rechtshaffen, Michael. "Review: *The Craft*." *Hollywood Reporter*, May 1, 1996, pp. 6, 9.

Richards, Jane. "Back from the Dead." *The Guardian*, April 24, 1998.

Rottenberg, Josh. "Neve Screams Again." *US*, September 1997.

Royce, Brenda Scott. *Party of Five: The Unofficial Companion*. Los Angeles: Renaissance Books, 1997.

Rusoff, Jane Wollman. "Neve Campbell." *Mr. Showbiz* Web site, December 12, 1997.

Schneller, Johanna. "Addicted to Love." *US*, February 1999, pp. 55–58.

Schwarzbaum, Lisa. "Shriek to Cheek." *Entertainment Weekly*, December 12, 1997, p. 49.

Scream Press Kit, Dimension Films, 1996.

Shaw, Jessica. "Reel World: Scream Dreams." *Entertainment Weekly*, January 15, 1999, p. 41.

Sheh, Stephanie. "Perennial Good Girl Neve Campbell Turns Bad in *Wild Things*." *University Wire*, March 19, 1998.

Slewinski, Christy. "Actress Doesn't Share Her Character's Angst." *New York Daily News*, September 2, 1996, p. 6C.

_____. "She Strays from the *Party* Line." *New York Daily News*, August 28, 1996, p. 75.

Snead, Elizabeth. "Fans Don't Have to Wait for Hewitt." *USA Today*, June 9, 1998, p. 8D.

Snierson, Dan. "Life of the Party." *Entertainment Weekly*, February 14, 1997, pp. 16–27.

Spelling, Ian. "The Fright Stuff." *Total TV*, January 17, 1997.

Stewart, Carolyn. "Hi, It's Neve Calling . . ." *Australian TV Week*, May 1997.

Strauss, Bob. "Review: *Scream*." *Los Angeles Daily News*, December 20, 1996, p. 9.

Svetkey, Benjamin. "Interview with a Vamp." *Entertainment Weekly*, April 10, 1998, p. 32.

_____. "Spring Movie Preview." *Entertainment Weekly*, February 20, 1998, p. 38.

Thomas, Kevin. "Good vs. Evil in Clever, Gruesome *Craft*." *Los Angeles Times*, May 3, 1996, p. F16.

_____. "Review: *Scream*." *Los Angeles Times*, December 20, 1996, p. 14.

_____. "Well, You'd *Scream* Too." *Los Angeles Times*, December 12, 1997, p. F1.

Thompson, Bob. "Enough to Make Campbell *Scream*." *Toronto Sun*, December 11, 1997.

_____. "L.A. Life a Scream for Neve Campbell." *Toronto Sun*, December 12, 1996.

Thompson, Malissa. "Neve Campbell." *Seventeen*, October 1995, p. 89.

Turan, Kenneth. "Stepping into Lethargic World of *54*." *Los Angeles Times*, August 28, 1998, p. F2.

Vanstone, Ellen. "Simply Stunning." *Canadian TV Guide*, August 17, 1996.

Vincent, Mal. "Neve Campbell Has Her Life Set in Career Mode." (Quincy, Massachusetts) *Patriot Ledger,* April 11, 1998.

Weeks, Janet. "Hollywood Is Seeing Teen." *USA Today*, December 22, 1997.

_____. "Screen Gems: TV's Young." *USA Today*, March 18, 1998, p. 1D.

_____. "Young Actresses Take a Walk on the Wild Side." *USA Today*, March 20, 1998, p. 13E.

Weiner, Sherry. "Neve Campbell." *UniverCity*, December 1997.

Weinraub, Bernard. "For Scream, a Good Scare Goes a Long Way." *New York Times*, June 12, 1997, pp. B1, B7.

_____. "Neve Campbell: Red Hot Right Now." *Cosmopolitan*, January 1997, pp. 80–81.

"Where Life Is Always a Beach." *People*, July 17, 1998, p. 18.

Wolf, Jeanne. "Neve Campbell Gets on Her Toes." TV Guide Online (www.tvguide.com), June 23, 1998.

Wyatt, Gene. "Neve Campbell's Game Growing So Fast, It's Almost Scary." *Tennessean*, December 17, 1997.

Index

Born in Kiev, Ukraine, on April 26, 1973, Elina Furman grew up in Highland Park, Illinois. Upon graduating from the University of Illinois with a B.A. in English literature, she worked as a senior editor at the Nightingale Conant Corp. and a media spokesperson for Quicken software. She currently lives and works in New York City. Her first book, *The Everything After College Book*, was published in 1998, and she has since written numerous books, including *The James Van Der Beek Story* (1999), *Ricky Martin* (1999), *98 Degrees* (1999), *The Everything Dating Book* (1999), *Heart of Soul: The Lauryn Hill Story* (1999), and *Generation Inc.: 100 Best Business Ideas for Young Entrepreneurs* (2000). She is also a contributing writer for *Daily Variety*.